# 50 Walks in

# LANCASHIRE
# & CHESHIRE

First published 2003
Researched and written by Jon Sparks

Produced by AA Publishing
© Automobile Association Developments Limited 2003
Illustrations © Automobile Association Developments Limited 2003

Published by AA Publishing (a trading name of Automobile
Association Developments Limited, whose registered office is
Millstream, Maidenhead, Windsor, SL4 5GD;
registered number 1878835)

**Ordnance Survey®** This product includes mapping data licensed from
Ordnance Survey® with the permission of the
Controller of Her Majesty's Stationery Office.
© Crown copyright 2003. All rights reserved. Licence number 399221

ISBN 0 7495 3562 8

A1231

A CIP catalogue record for this book is available
from the British Library.

The contents of this book are believed correct at the time of printing.
Nevertheless, the publishers cannot be held responsible for any errors
or omissions or for changes in the details given in this book or for
the consequences of any reliance on the information it provides. This
does not affect your statutory rights. We have tried to ensure
accuracy in this book, but things do change and we would be grateful
if readers would advise us of any inaccuracies they may encounter.

We have taken all reasonable steps to ensure that these walks are
safe and achievable by walkers with a realistic level of fitness.
However, all outdoor activities involve a degree of risk and the
publishers accept no responsibility for any injuries caused to
readers whilst following these walks. For more advice on walking
safely see page 128. The mileage range shown on the front cover is for
guidance only – some walks may exceed or be less than these
distances.

Visit the AA Publishing website at www.theAA.com

Paste-up and editorial by Outcrop Publishing Services Ltd, Cumbria
for AA Publishing

Colour reproduction by LC Repro
Printed in Italy by G Canale & C SPA, Torino, Italy

# Legend

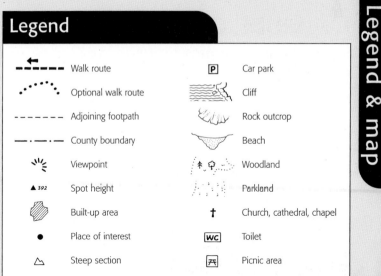

| | | | |
|---|---|---|---|
| ← – – – – – | Walk route | P | Car park |
| •••••••• | Optional walk route | Cliff | Cliff |
| – – – – – – | Adjoining footpath | Rock outcrop | Rock outcrop |
| – · – · – · – | County boundary | Beach | Beach |
| Viewpoint | Viewpoint | Woodland | Woodland |
| ▲ 392 | Spot height | Parkland | Parkland |
| Built-up area | Built-up area | † | Church, cathedral, chapel |
| ● | Place of interest | WC | Toilet |
| △ | Steep section | 禾 | Picnic area |

# Lancashire & Cheshire locator map

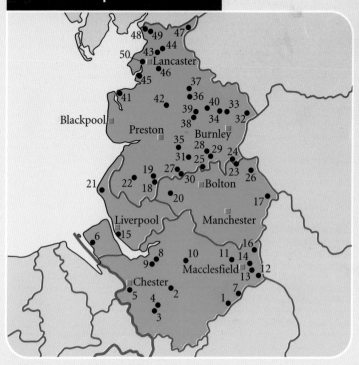

Contents

Contents

| WALK | RATING | DISTANCE | PAGE |
|------|--------|----------|------|

**Rating:** Each walk is rated for its relative difficulty compared to the other walks in this book. Walks marked 🚶🚶 🚶🚶 🚶🚶 are likely to be shorter and easier with little total ascent. The hardest walks are marked 🚶🚶 🚶🚶 🚶🚶 .

**Walking in Safety:** For advice and safety tips ➤ 128.

# Introducing Lancashire & Cheshire

In 1974 we were told that the 'new' counties were purely administrative and wouldn't sweep away historical identities. It doesn't seem to have worked that way. It's hard to remember that, only a generation ago, Liverpool and Manchester were both in Lancashire, as was a good chunk of the Lake District. Boundaries change, and so do landscapes. The landscapes of this region bear the imprint of millennia of human activity. Chester was a great Roman centre, but Lancashire something of a backwater. Until a century after the Norman Conquest it was ruled partly from Cheshire and partly from Yorkshire. It gained wealth and importance slowly through the following centuries.

From the middle of the 18th century, accelerating change reshaped the face of the region and made it the centre of developments that rippled out across the entire world. Within the span of a single human life canals, railways and steam-powered factories all made their first appearance. The world's first commercial railway, between Liverpool and Manchester, opened in 1830. Only 14 years later regular trains were running between London and Lancaster. During the Industrial Revolution, the region had a significance at least as great as Silicon Valley today.

Yet, only a few miles from these hotbeds of change, large areas remained sparsely populated and seemingly untouched. Most of Cheshire, and most of present-day Lancashire, is open country, from the high moors to the pastures and arable fields. The classic English landscape of hedges, woods and fields survives better in Cheshire and Lancashire than in many other shires. However, we shouldn't imagine that this landscape is 'timeless'. It's a creation of an agricultural revolution that ran parallel with industrial change.

That these changes happened at the same time is no coincidence. Agricultural developments made the industrial ones possible. Areas like the Cheshire Plain and West Lancashire played a vital role in feeding the expanding towns. Potatoes, imported from the New World, were soon a staple. Fish (from Fleetwood) and chips (from Pilling or Ormskirk potatoes) is another tradition that began around this time.

If these areas fed the workers, then Lancaster and Liverpool fed the mills with imported cotton. Stone was quarried from the hills and coal from under the fields. The story of the region is one of change, but change is not a one-way street. There are new

---

**PUBLIC TRANSPORT** ⓘ

The region is well covered by public transport. Nearly all the walks can be reached using either buses or trains, and it's especially appropriate for the more urban walks. Sometimes it will be logical to start the walk at a different point on the circuit. There's comprehensive telephone information on 0870 6082608, while National Rail Enquiries are on 08457 48 49 50. On the Internet try www.totaljourney.com.

towns growing, like Topsy, and empty valleys where hundreds or thousands once lived. Areas which were once intensively farmed are now empty moorland. Old quarries are colonised by rock climbers, and by peregrine falcons. Of the numerous railway lines that closed in the 1960s, most are now invaluable for walkers and cyclists. Canals have traded commerce for pleasure-boating, angling, wildlife and of course for walking. These layers of history add fascination to most of the walks. You can delve into industrial archaeology or see how 'abandoned' sites often provide a richer habitat for wildlife than modern farming allows.

Still, when you really want to get away from it all, there are always places touched by wildness; dragonfly-haunted wetlands, ancient woodlands, hidden valleys and rocky ridges. Above all, there are the vast moors. An old music chimes in the names of beck and fell, and there's music older still in the curlew's bubbling cry, drifting across skylines that haven't changed since the ice age.

# Using this Book

## Information panels
An information panel for each walk shows its relative difficulty (► 5), the distance and total amount of ascent. An indication of the gradients you will encounter is shown by the rating ▲▲▲ (no steep slopes) to ▲▲▲ (several very steep slopes).

## Maps
There are 30 maps, covering 40 of the walks. Some walks have a suggested option in the same area. The information panel for these walks will tell you how much extra walking is involved. On short-cut suggestions the panel will tell you the total distance if you set out from the start of the main walk. Where an option returns to the same point on the main walk, just the distance of the loop is given. Where an option leaves the main walk at one point and returns to it at another, then the distance shown is for the whole walk. The minimum time suggested is for reasonably fit walkers and doesn't allow for stops. Each walk has a suggested map. Laminated aqua3 maps are longer lasting and water resistant.

## Start Points
The start of each walk is given as a six-figure grid reference prefixed by two letters indicating which 100km square of the National Grid it refers to. You'll find more information on grid references on most Ordnance Survey maps.

## Dogs
We have tried to give dog owners useful advice about how dog friendly each walk is. Please respect other countryside users. Keep your dog under control, especially around livestock, and obey local bylaws and other dog control notices.

## Car Parking
Many of the car parks suggested are public, but occasionally you may find you have to park on the roadside or in a lay-by. Please be considerate when you leave your car, ensuring that access roads or gates are not blocked and that other vehicles can pass safely. Remember that pub car parks are private and should not be used unless you have the owner's permission.

**Walk 1**

# Down and Up Again to Mow Cop

*A walk that samples both the lush Cheshire Plain and the wilder ridges that overlook it.*

| | |
|---|---|
| •DISTANCE• | 5¼ miles (8.4km) |
| •MINIMUM TIME• | 2hrs |
| •ASCENT / GRADIENT• | 720ft (219m) ▲▲▲ |
| •LEVEL OF DIFFICULTY• | 🚶🚶 🚶🚶 🚶🚶 |
| •PATHS• | Open fields and woodland paths, canal tow path, quiet lanes, short sections where path indistinct, 10 stiles |
| •LANDSCAPE• | Mostly farmland and deciduous woods on flanks of ridge, views from crest |
| •SUGGESTED MAP• | aqua3 OS Explorer 268 Wilmslow, Macclesfield & Congleton |
| •START / FINISH• | Grid reference: SJ 857573 |
| •DOG FRIENDLINESS• | Woods and canal tow path are best places to let dogs run |
| •PARKING• | National Trust car park directly below Mow Cop castle |
| •PUBLIC TOILETS• | In nearby towns of Kidsgrove or Biddulph |

## BACKGROUND TO THE WALK

Some people might think it odd to start a walk on the top of a hill, descend, and then climb up again, but then Mow Cop is an odd place. Its crooked streets seem positively to seek the steepest ways. Split between the two counties of Cheshire and Staffordshire, the village is as quirky as the castle that dominates it. Never a fortress, the castle was built principally for embellishment and remains one of England's best-known and most conspicuous follies.

### View From a Hill
It's not the view to it that concerns us, however, so much as the view from. Mow Cop is perched on a sharp ridge, the last great outlier of the millstone grit. The view south is over the Potteries but north and west is the green expanse of the Cheshire Plain. The distinct boundary between hill and plain is underlined by the Macclesfield Canal.

The walk starts level, passing the Old Man of Mow. Logic suggests that this monolith is merely an incidental remnant left behind when the quarries closed. Yet it's so sculpted that you can't help feeling that, consciously or not, there was some artistry at work here. This is a good place to pause and study the view before descending to the plain.

### Speed
The descent is steepest in the woods of Roe Park. Down on the level, you first cross the main Manchester-to-Stoke-on-Trent railway line. Take care as high speed trains use this line. Just beyond, and on a parallel course, is the Macclesfield Canal, where the speed limit is a sedate 4mph (6.4kph). Though the general line of the canal was planned by Thomas Telford, the principal engineer was William Crossley.

**The Path Vanishes**

On the way up again, you need to be alert for a short section in the woods past Limekiln Farm. The path tries to hide in the undergrowth, then doubles back sharply as if trying to shake off pursuit. Higher up, there's a section with no clear path at all, but it's simply a matter of following the edge of a field.

Overall the ascent is less steep than the descent, but there's rough ground below the ridge crest. Here, if you so desire, you can walk with one foot in Cheshire and the other in Staffordshire. A path then threads a narrow belt of woodland before emerging into another old quarry. No Old Men here, but in summer the level floor is alive with wild flowers.

## Walk 1 Directions

① Head towards the castle. Before reaching it take a narrower path left, to a road. Go right up this, then left, signposted 'Old Man' and 'South Cheshire Way'. Swing left, then right, then fork right on a narrow path past the **Old Man**. Rejoin the wider track, heading towards a communications mast.

② At a junction of footpaths go left. Follow the field edges downhill and continue descending in a wood. Where the footpath splits at a tangle of holly bushes go left and into a

**Walk 1**

### WHILE YOU'RE THERE ⓘ
**Little Moreton Hall**, which you can see from the ridge, is almost certainly the most celebrated half-timbered house in England. The house was built in stages between 1480 and 1580 and has hardly changed since. From the classic views of the exterior reflected in the moat to the wall decorations inside, everything is a striking expression of its time.

field, then bear right. Skirt a farm then join a rough track. Keep heading downhill to join a surfaced lane. Bear left and cross the railway at **Ackers Crossing**.

③ Follow the lane to a wider road and turn right. Cross over a canal bridge, then go down steps and left, along the tow path. At **bridge No 81** go up to a lane and turn left, over the bridge.

④ Follow the narrow lane to a crossroads by **Baytree Farm** and go straight ahead up the track to **Limekiln Farm**. Take a track on the left just beyond the buildings. Keep low, along the edge of the wood, until the track bends right by a post marked with yellow arrows.

⑤ Go left, pushing through undergrowth to duckboards and a stile. Turn right along a field edge. After 100yds (91m) there's another post. Descend sharp right then cross several, sometimes slippery,

plank bridges. A narrow path heads uphill leading to a wider track, then tarmac near a house. Before the track starts to descend again, go right to a stile. Follow the left edge of a field alongside a wood. After another stile go up a narrower field until it opens out. Above a signpost, go right on a green track to a stile amid holly trees. Continue to another boundary; beyond is rougher ground with rushes and some gorse. A firm track curves across this, though the last bit, to a stile remains rough and rushy. Bear left up a drive to the road, then follow it right for 300yds (274m).

### WHERE TO EAT AND DRINK ⓘ
The **Mow Cop Inn** is close at hand, just below the hilltop on the Staffordshire side. It's a cosy pub with a local feel that does good-value food, but isn't open all day. For a wider range of options, including no-smoking areas, try the **Egerton Arms** at Astbury, just off the A34 near Congleton.

⑥ By a gateway on the right-hand side a Gritstone Trail sign lurks under a beech tree, pointing the way into a narrow wood. The footpath roughly follows the upper margin of the wood, then emerges on the level floor of some old quarry workings. Bear left, below the communications tower, to rejoin the outward route near the **Old Man of Mow**.

### WHAT TO LOOK FOR ⓘ
**Mow Cop folly** was built in 1754 by John and Ralph Harding for the Wilbraham family of Rode Hall, about 3 miles (4.8km) to the west. It was probably used as an occasional summerhouse, but mostly served to enhance the view from Rode Hall. The hilltop was also the birthplace of Primitive Methodism: in May 1807 thousands gathered to launch a move back to simpler forms of worship. The term 'primitive' was not seen as derogatory: the usual contemporary term of abuse was 'Ranters'.

# Woods and Heaths of Little Budworth

*An easy walk centred around the distinctive heathland of Little Budworth Country Park.*

| | |
|---|---|
| **•DISTANCE•** | 3½ miles (5.7km) |
| **•MINIMUM TIME•** | 1hr 15min |
| **•ASCENT / GRADIENT•** | 98ft (30m) |
| **•LEVEL OF DIFFICULTY•** | |
| **•PATHS•** | Easy tracks at first, field paths and some (usually quiet) road walking, 14 stiles |
| **•LANDSCAPE•** | Mature woodland, open heath, farmland and mere |
| **•SUGGESTED MAP•** | aqua3 OS Explorer 267 Northwich & Delamere Forest |
| **•START / FINISH•** | Grid reference: SJ 590654 |
| **•DOG FRIENDLINESS•** | Can run free in country park and fenced track |
| **•PARKING•** | Main car park for Little Budworth Country Park |
| **•PUBLIC TOILETS•** | At start |

## BACKGROUND TO THE WALK

In the middle of all the rich green farmland of lowland Cheshire is an island of something different, a little piece of a rougher, older landscape. As ever, though, to call it 'wild' would be misleading. There is probably no such thing as a truly wild landscape anywhere in England. Usually it's peaceful, but a word of warning – it is very close to the Oulton Park motor-racing circuit. On race days not only is the traffic abominable, there's no escaping the noise either.

**Lowland Heath**

The area now called Little Budworth Country Park is a fragment of lowland heath. Britain has a substantial proportion of the world's lowland heath, but there is a lot less than there used to be – only 18 per cent of what was recorded in 1800. Most of what remains is in Southern England, so all in all, Little Budworth is a bit special.

The essence of heath is an open landscape, with a mix of heather, gorse, bracken and grasses and with only scattered, if any, trees. Gorse is unmistakable and in summer the popping of its seed pods makes it one of those rare plants you can recognise with your ears. There are two characteristic species of heather: ling (which gardeners may know as *Calluna vulgaris*) and bell heather (*Erica cinerea*). They often grow together and look quite similar, but ling has slightly paler and more open flowers.

Heathland typically developed from areas cleared of trees from neolithic times onward, as the poor soil made it unsuitable for permanent cultivation. The land was, however, still used for grazing. Gorse was traditionally used as fuel and for animal fodder, while bracken provided animal bedding and was also a valuable source of potash. These activities, and the occasional natural fire, prevented the heath reverting to woodland. Much of today's country park is wooded, but you will also see large areas of heath, including some which have recently been cleared.

**The Margins of Budworth Mere**

The majority of the heathland at Little Budworth is dry, but there are some low-lying wetter areas. The pool that you pass on the walk is a great breeding ground for dragonflies and damselflies. By contrast the second half of the walk crosses farmland and then skirts the reedy margins of Budworth Mere. Many of Cheshire's meres were created by subsidence resulting from salt mining. Such relatively new lakes are also often called 'flashes'. Others, like this one, are natural in origin, formed in hollows in the lumpy mantle of 'drift' left by retreating ice at the end of the last ice age.

Finally the walk visits Little Budworth village. It is peaceful and attractive but not so outrageously pretty that it has become a tourist magnet. You'll probably agree that this is to its benefit.

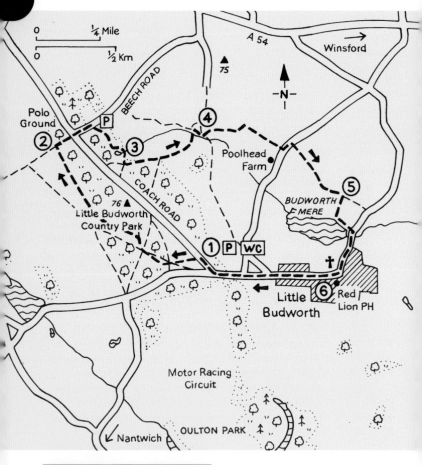

## Walk 2 Directions

① Go straight across the **Coach Road** to a path then turn right on a wider path. Fork left and follow the main path, keeping straight on at a crossroads, with a Heathland Trail sign, and again at the next crossing. When a field appears ahead, follow the path alongside to its right. This veers away right. Go back left just before a cleared area, by another Heathland Trail marker.

**Walk 2**

② Go right on a wide track to the **Coach Road** and straight across into **Beech Road**. After 230yds (210m) enter a small car park. Near its far end is a signboard with a map. Go through a gap in the fence beside this. The path skirts a depression with a boggy pool, then curves round a larger pool.

③ Cross a causeway/dam by the pool and gently climb a sunken track beyond. As it levels out, fork left by a Heathland Trail sign then turn left, with an open field not far away to the left. Bear left on a wider surfaced track, swinging down past an ornamental pool in a dip. Immediately after this turn right on a sandy track.

④ Where another path crosses, most people evidently go through a gate ahead into the corner of the field. Strictly speaking, however, the right of way goes over a stile to its right then across the (very wet and smelly) corner of a wood to a second stile. From here bear right

under a power line, to a stile in the far corner. Follow a narrow path (beware nettles), then over a stile on the right and straight across a large field. Aim just left of the farm to a gate and stile. Go left on a lane for 60yds (55m) then right down a track. This becomes narrower, then descends slightly.

⑤ As it levels out, there's a stile on the right, with a sign for **Budworth Mere**. Go down towards the water then left on a path skirting the mere. At the end go right up a road, swinging further right into the centre of **Little Budworth**.

⑥ Keep straight on along the road, through the village then past open fields. Opposite the entrance gates of **Oulton Park** is the start of the **Coach Road**. Follow this, or the parallel footpath to its left for 125yds (114m), to the car park.

**Walk 3**

# Views of Cheshire's Castle Country

*A loop walk on the most accessible section of a prominent sandstone ridge.*

| | |
|---|---|
| •DISTANCE• | 5½ miles (8.8km) |
| •MINIMUM TIME• | 2hrs |
| •ASCENT / GRADIENT• | 919ft (280m) ▲▲▲ |
| •LEVEL OF DIFFICULTY• | 👫 👫 👫 |
| •PATHS• | Field and woodland paths, plus some lane walking, 9 stiles (currently being replaced by gates) |
| •LANDSCAPE• | Richly varied woodland and farmland, some rocky outcrops and views over lush plains |
| •SUGGESTED MAP• | aqua3 OS Explorer 257 Crewe & Nantwich |
| •START / FINISH• | Grid reference: SJ 520550 |
| •DOG FRIENDLINESS• | On leads in Peckforton Estate and near grazing stock. Beware of electric fences |
| •PARKING• | Verges at end of tarmac on Coppermines Lane, off A534 |
| •PUBLIC TOILETS• | None on route |

## BACKGROUND TO THE WALK

Beeston Castle, visible from afar, was built in the 13th century, its strategic hilltop site looking towards the turbulent Welsh border. It saw no real battles until the English Civil War around 400 years later. After changing hands several times, it was largely demolished in 1646 on Parliament's orders. Nearby Peckforton Castle is a 19th-century imitation of a medieval fortress.

### Layers of History

Distant views of these castle-crowned ridges might lead you to anticipate airy ridge walking. In fact there's little of that to be found here, though Raw Head Hill does provide some moments of drama. Generally, however, this walk delivers something different and equally pleasurable.

The castles proclaim the long history of the area, but there are other layers of history to be found. The name of Coppermines Lane, where the walk starts, is a reminder of an industrial element. Where the walk first leaves the tarmac, a chimney glimpsed below marks the site of the old copper works. Just above, the map still marks the site of a mine, though there's little to be seen of it now.

### Sandstone Trail

From here the way climbs to Raw Head Hill, along a steep slope which breaks into startling crags at Musket's Hole. The summit, at 746ft (227m), is the highest point on the Sandstone Trail, a 34-mile (55km) route from Frodsham (▶ Walk 8) to Whitchurch. However, a screen of trees means it's far from the best viewpoint. The walk does serve up some great views, but never an all-round panorama: more a series of tasty morsels than a grand main course. But there's charm in their sudden and often fleeting appearance.

Walk 3

## High Point

After Raw Head Hill the walk winds down through woods, fields and a quiet lane to Burwardsley village then up an even quieter one to Higher Burwardsley. Then it climbs again to the National Trust-owned Bulkeley Hill Wood. The high point, literally and metaphorically, is a wonderful grove of sweet chestnut trees on a broad shelf rimmed by low sandstone crags. With virtually no undergrowth, you can fully appreciate the gnarled, multistemmed trees, which seem hunched with age. From here it's an easy stroll down through a plantation and then across a field back to Coppermines Lane.

## Walk 3 **Directions**

① Walk down **Coppermines Lane** to a sharp left-hand bend then over a stile beside an arched sandstone overhang. Cross a field then ascend the edge of a wooded area. Cross fields to the edge of another wood. Go up right, joining a track towards **Chiflik Farm**.

② Go through a kissing gate by the farm and up a fenced path. The path generally runs just below the top of a steep slope, gradually climbing to the trig point on **Raw Head Hill**.

---

**WHILE YOU'RE THERE**  ⓘ

Peckforton Castle isn't open to visitors, but **Beeston Castle** is – and to the elements too. Much of it is in ruins, apart from the gatehouse and some towers of the outer wall. Its condition seems perfectly fitting for the atmospheric site.

---

③ The path goes right and into a slight dip. Go left down steps then back right, slanting through a steep plantation. Go left down a narrow lane for 300yds (274m). Opposite a track and footpath sign, descend rightwards on clear ground under tall trees. At the bottom cross a stile and go up towards **Bodnook Cottage**. Just below this bear left and into a wood. Follow a much clearer path, roughly level then slightly left and downhill among spindly beech trees.

④ Cross a stile at the edge of the wood, then another immediately to its right. There's no path, so aim directly for a stile below a large tree, 50yds (46m) left of a house. The path is clearer through the next field. At the end cross a stile and follow the road ahead.

⑤ On the edge of **Burwardsley** village turn right up the first lane. Go right again up **Sarra Lane**, then fork left at an 'Unsuitable for Motor Vehicles' sign. Follow the lane through a narrow section then past **Cheshire Workshops**. Just beyond this the road forks.

---

**WHAT TO LOOK FOR**  ⓘ

**Sweet chestnuts**, like those in Bulkeley Hill Wood, are not a native species; they probably arrived with the Romans. Nor are they closely related to the horse chestnut, which gets its name from the chance resemblance of its fruit. In fact the sweet chestnut is related to the oaks.

---

⑥ Go right then straight on up the hill. Keep right at the next fork. The lane becomes unsurfaced at the Crewe and Nantwich boundary.

⑦ Just before you get to the boundary sign go right over a stile and follow a clear path down the edge of a field. Keep straight on until you meet a narrow lane and go up left. On the crest, opposite a gatehouse, go right on a track.

⑧ Go left up steps into the wood and continue less steeply. Where the path splits, the left branch follows the brink of a steep slope. Keep fairly close to this edge as the path levels. Go through a gap in a fence then descend straight ahead, through a plantation, to a kissing gate alongside a big iron gate. Go diagonally right on a clear track across a field to **Coppermines Lane**.

---

**WHERE TO EAT AND DRINK**  ⓘ

The **Pheasant Inn**, in Higher Burwardsley, is only a few paces from the route. There's outdoor seating with an excellent view, real ale and good food. After the walk, try the **Bickerton Poacher** on the A534 near Coppermines Lane.

# On Peckforton's Estate

*More classic Cheshire farmland and richly varied woods.*
**See map and information panel for Walk 3**

| | |
|---|---|
| •**DISTANCE**• | 8½ miles (13.7km) |
| •**MINIMUM TIME**• | 2hrs 45min |
| •**ASCENT / GRADIENT**• | 1,200ft (366m) ▲▲▲ |
| •**LEVEL OF DIFFICULTY**• | 🚶 🚶 🚶 |

## Walk 4 Directions (Walk 3 option)

At the fork (Point ⑥) keep left, then go straight across the crossroads into **Pennsylvania Lane**, passing the **Pheasant Inn**. Follow the lane for 350yds (320m) to a stile on the left under a large oak tree. Follow the hedge down to a stile in the corner, then slant down to a concealed stile in the bottom corner of the next field.

Turn right down the lane. Just inside the entrance of **Outlanes Farm** (Point Ⓐ) go right, over stiles skirting the farm, then left behind the large shed. Cross a small footbridge and go up right to the next stile. Bear left past a cattle trough, to a tree on the rise and then down to a gap in the hedge, directly in line with the large farm.

At the edge of the farm compound (Point Ⓑ) cross a stile by an iron gate and double back along the edge of the field. This section gives a classic view of Beeston Castle on its crag-fringed hilltop.

Cross a small footbridge and keep straight on up a short slope. Pass right of a dew pond to the next stile, in a broken hedge line. Though quite new, this stile appears redundant – except when there's an electric fence along this boundary!

Keep parallel to the edge of wood to another stile, then bear right to a small footbridge. Just beyond is a signpost. Follow a cleared line through crops to another fingerpost (Point Ⓒ) and go left along the track. This becomes a lane lined with cottages, many in distinctive Peckforton Estate livery and eminently photogenic.

Just past **Oak Cottage**, go sharp right on a track through woods. The gentle gradient gives a painless ascent for nearly a mile (1.6km). As the track starts to descend (Point Ⓓ) fork left on a narrower path, with a Sandstone Trail sign. The path climbs across a very steep slope, decorated with sandstone outcrops and tree roots. At the crest, ignore the stile ahead and go down to the right, through a gate, then follow a path alongside a wall.

Keep straight ahead, to a stile on the bend of a narrow lane, and go left. In 100yds (91m) you reach a T-junction and rejoin Walk 3. Go up left, and the Crewe and Nantwich boundary sign (Point ⑦) is 50yds (46m) ahead.

Walk 5

# Chester's Walls and Water

*The classic circuit of Chester's medieval walls, with a few variations.*

| | |
|---|---|
| •DISTANCE• | 2¾ miles (4.4km) |
| •MINIMUM TIME• | 1hr |
| •ASCENT / GRADIENT• | 164ft (50m) ▲▲▲▲ |
| •LEVEL OF DIFFICULTY• | 🚶 🚶 🚶 |
| •PATHS• | Pavements and surfaced paths |
| •LANDSCAPE• | Historic but crowded urban scene, racecourse and river |
| •SUGGESTED MAP• | aqua3 OS Explorer 266 Wirral & Chester |
| •START / FINISH• | Grid reference: SJ 407664 |
| •DOG FRIENDLINESS• | Unlikely to feel welcome on streets and narrow wall path |
| •PARKING• | Park-and-Ride at Upton and on A548, A483 and A41 |
| •PUBLIC TOILETS• | On Frodsham Street and at Chester Visitor Centre |

## Walk 5 Directions

From Frodsham Street, turn right into **Foregate Street** then under the clock into **Eastgate Street** and along to High Cross. Turn right on to **Northgate Street**. Where it opens out turn left through a gap into **Hamilton Place**. In 20yds (18m), on the right, a large glass window shows the strongroom of the Roman headquarters or Principia.

Return to Northgate Street and continue to the grand Town Hall of 1869. Turn right under the 14th-century Abbey Gate into Georgian **Abbey Square**. In the corner there's an entrance to the cathedral. Its exterior is largely Victorian but much of the older fabric can still be seen inside. Leave the square by **Abbey Street** and go up on to the walls. Turn left past the **Deanery Field**, to the Phoenix or King Charles Tower, where Charles I watched his army's heavy defeat at the Battle of Rowton Moor. Follow the walls round, overlooking the deep cutting of the Shropshire

Union Canal. As you reach Northgate Bridge, on the right is the Bluecoat School, founded in 1717 to counter 'the growth of vice and debauchery in Chester.'

Continue to another tower, **Morgan's Mount**. Descend steps on the left, loop round through the arch and descend to canal level. To your right is the cutting, carved in solid sandstone. Go left along the tow path to **Northgate Locks**. This unusual 'staircase lock' comes with full instructions for its use. The total drop is 33ft (10m). Below the locks the canal squeezes under the railway bridge, then the path forks.

Follow the tow path round under another bridge to **Northgate Basin**. Just across the water is Telford's warehouse, with its arched loading

### WHAT TO LOOK FOR ⓘ

There are numerous **metal plaques** around the walls. Excellent design and text that's both entertaining and informative mean they are not to be missed with little human stories bringing dry, historical facts to life.

dock. Return to the fork, go up to railings then turn left up steps and back to the walls. Turn right to **Bonewaldesthorne's Tower**, which guarded the harbour until the river changed its course.

The Water Tower and connecting wall were built in 1332 to maintain protection for the port. There's a good view here of the railway. This section of line into North Wales was built in 1846. Lines from an 1856 guidebook, quoted on a wall plaque, suggest how railways were viewed: 'Whew! With a rush like that of a tiger from his den … Full 40 miles an hour.'

> ### WHILE YOU'RE THERE ⓘ
> There's loads more to see, including shopping on the unique first-floor galleries of the **Rows**. You can learn a lot more about Chester's past from the hands-on re-creations of **The Deva Roman Experience**.

Continue down **City Walls Road**; the top of the wall is level with the road for a stretch. Pass the Queen's School then take the higher level, over **Watergate Bridge**. Just beyond this there's a good view of Chester Racecourse, said to be Britain's first. The course occupies an area called the Roodee, once a tidal pool, but silted up by medieval times.

Cross busy **Grosvenor Road** at the traffic lights to the continuation of the walls below Chester Castle. The medieval castle was replaced by a series of Greek revival buildings in the 1790s. When the walls sink to road level, cross to a path overlooking the river. Cross the **Dee Bridge**, with its pioneering hydro-electric station from 1913. Turn left along the far bank, past ugly modern flats and a restored

waterwheel, to **Queen's Park**. Go up steps and recross the river by Queen's Park Bridge. It was built in 1923 and bounces gently as you walk across.

Climb steps above the end of the bridge and 20yds (18m) further on turn left through a gate to the ruins of St John's Church, Chester's first cathedral. Continue along the side of the 19th-century church and round its west front to emerge alongside the remains of the Roman amphitheatre. It is the largest amphitheatre in Britain, with walls once 35ft (10m) high, though it's hard to imagine how it could hold 7,000 spectators.

Just beyond, on the left, are the Roman Gardens. They actually date from the 1950s, but do contain a collection of Roman masonry. Go under the arch of **Newgate** and turn left immediately on **Park Street**, past an unforgivable multi-storey car park to the graceful almshouses known as Nine Houses (there used to be more). Go up a ramp on to the walls and go left over Newgate.

Continue along the walls past the glass-cased remains of Thimbleby's Tower and on to the 18th-century **Eastgate**, surmounted by the elaborate clock erected to mark Queen Victoria's Diamond Jubilee. Just beyond, descend steps on the right to complete the circuit.

> ### WHERE TO EAT AND DRINK ⓘ
> There's no shortage of choice – two pubs and two cafés near Queen's Park Bridge offer riverside settings. For something special, however, go for the **Albion** on Park Street. Proudly declaring itself 'family-hostile', and with Christmas decorations up all year, it seems to exist in a time warp.

**Walk 6**

# Uncommon Delights at Thurstaston

*Panoramic views from a heathland crest, and the edge of a grand estuary.*

| | |
|---|---|
| **·DISTANCE·** | 5¼ miles (8.4km) |
| **·MINIMUM TIME·** | 1hr 45min |
| **·ASCENT / GRADIENT·** | 345ft (105m) ▲▲▲ |
| **·LEVEL OF DIFFICULTY·** | 🚶 🚶 🚶 |
| **·PATHS·** | Some road walking, sandy tracks and bare rock, then field paths, 2 stiles |
| **·LANDSCAPE·** | Woodland and heath, farmland, seashore |
| **·SUGGESTED MAP·** | aqua3 OS Explorer 266 Wirral & Chester |
| **·START / FINISH·** | Grid reference: SJ 238834 |
| **·DOG FRIENDLINESS·** | Dogs have several opportunities to roam |
| **·PARKING·** | Wirral Country Park at bottom of Station Road, Thurstaston |
| **·PUBLIC TOILETS·** | In Country Park Visitor Centre adjacent to car park |

## BACKGROUND TO THE WALK

This is a walk of two distinct halves. It's somewhat unfortunate that the busy A540 underlines this division, but not that there's so much variety in a small space. You start near to the shoreline but, saving that for the end, climb long straight Station Road. This is an uninspiring opening but easy and quick. The grand Church of St Bartholomew signals the end of the beginning and once the main road is crossed you're on Thurstaston Common.

### Thurstaston Common

Many people expect 'common' to be open but the name really refers to common grazing. Where this right is no longer exercised, unless the land is managed in some way, it's quite normal for it to revert to woodland. In fact most of the common is wooded but there are still good open stretches where heathland survives. It's obviously difficult for trees to gain a foothold in the thin sandy soils of the more exposed parts.

Most of the ground is dry but there are a few damper hollows. One such hollow is skirted early on. In summer it's marked by the white tassels of cotton grass. The wet patches are also home to cross-leaved heath, not the ling and bell heather of the drier areas. Its flowers grow in clusters rather than spikes. Also found are sundews, low-growing plants with reddish, hairy, sticky leaves. These trap insects from which the plant gains nutrients lacking in the poor soils.

Just below the summit you break out on to a bare sandstone crest which gives a view over the Dee Estuary and out to sea. On a clear day the Great Orme behind Llandudno stands out boldly. You might also spot a gas platform or two out in the Irish Sea. From the summit itself the view spreads to include the Liverpool cathedrals. The Forest of Bowland and Winter Hill rise to their left, and you can also identify Formby Point (► Walk 21).

After retracing your steps as far as the church, the second half of this walk begins innocuously across farmland, but as you descend towards the sea, there's an unexpected moment of drama as you arrive at the ravine of the Dungeon, complete with tiny waterfall.

Below this you join the old railway which is now the Wirral Way. Past ponds, home to water-lilies and moorhens, you soon reach the brink of the slope about 50ft (15m) above the estuary. It's stretching it a bit to call it a cliff, but it's steep enough to be no place to slip. There's little solid rock exposed in these 'cliffs', which are composed of boulder clay. This is nearly the end of the walk, but you may want to linger and savour the view across the wide estuary to Wales.

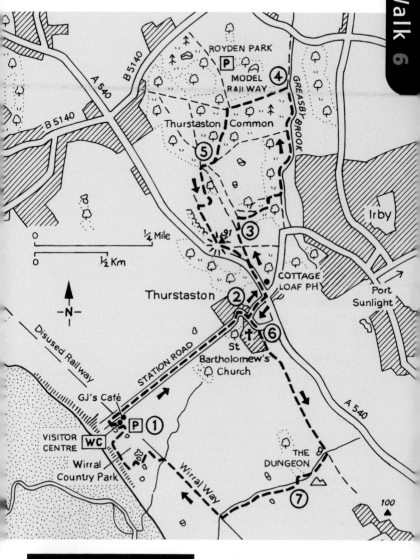

# Walk 6 **Directions**

① From the car park, loop round past the visitor centre and wildlife pond, go out to **Station Road** and

go straight up for ½ mile (800m). At the top it swings right.

② Turn left before the church and go up to the **A540**. Go left, past the **Cottage Loaf**, then go right through

**Walk 6**

a kissing gate. Follow the track straight ahead to the end of a cul-de-sac.

③ Go through a kissing gate to a broad path then go right on a smaller path. Cross a track near a cattle grid and take the left of two paths. This swings left and crosses a clearing. Go right to meet a clearer path just inside the edge of the wood. Go left, following the course of **Greasby Brook**.

④ A boundary wall appears ahead. Turn left alongside it. Where it ends keep straight on, passing the model railway. Alongside **Royden Park** the wall resumes. Where it ends again turn left by a sign and map. Cross a clearing to a junction.

⑤ Twenty yards (18m) further on is a kissing gate. Turn right before it, on a narrow path. Cross another path and plough through gorse for 20yds (18m) to a broader path. Go left then up past a marker stone, over tree roots and bare rock. Descend steps, pass a small pool, then ascend to a larger area of bare rock. Go right here and when the path forks, go left, then right, through a band of trees. Go left on a broad path to a sandstone pillar with a map/view indicator and then the trig point. Descend a broad path that rejoins the outward route. Retrace your steps past the **Cottage Loaf** and down the top section of **Station Road**.

⑥ Turn left past the church. When the road swings round to the left, a lane continues straight ahead. Cross a stile and follow a well-marked footpath. In a dip cross a stream and turn right at a footpath sign. After recrossing the stream, zig-zag down a steeper slope into **The Dungeon**.

⑦ Cross the stream again and follow it down. Climb on to an old railway embankment and go right. When green gates bar the way, sidestep left. Continue for another 220yds (201m) to a gap in the hedge. Follow a path, winding past a couple of ponds then out to the cliff tops above the estuary. Go right for 240yds (219m), then bear right across grass towards the visitor centre and the car park.

Walk 7

# Viewing The Cloud from Both Sides

*An exhilarating walk with a long, easy prelude then a steep ascent to one of Cheshire's best viewpoints.*

| | |
|---|---|
| •DISTANCE• | 7 miles (11.3km) |
| •MINIMUM TIME• | 2hrs 30min |
| •ASCENT / GRADIENT• | 804ft (245m) ▲▲▲ |
| •LEVEL OF DIFFICULTY• | 🚶 🚶 🚶 |
| •PATHS• | Field paths, canal tow path, some lanes, rougher and steeper on The Cloud, 11 stiles |
| •LANDSCAPE• | Meadows and fields along canal, craggy summit |
| •SUGGESTED MAP• | aqua3 OS Explorer 268 Wilmslow, Macclesfield & Congleton |
| •START / FINISH• | Grid reference: SJ 894627 |
| •DOG FRIENDLINESS• | Can run free on tow path and upper reaches of The Cloud |
| •PARKING• | Car park on outskirts of small village of Timbersbrook |
| •PUBLIC TOILETS• | At car park |

## BACKGROUND TO THE WALK

It's an enticing name, The Cloud, and the views from the crag-fringed crest live up to the promise. Instead of a direct attack this walk first makes a wide, easy sweep around the hill. This is attractive in its own right and gives you a greater feel for the landscape you'll ultimately survey.

### Along the Macclesfield Canal

Even so, a downhill start may seem perverse. In fact the height lost is minimal and the gains considerable. An early wander through flower-rich meadows may seem all too short. Easy striding follows, along the tow path of the Macclesfield Canal. Though it passes close to Congleton, you see surprisingly little of the town. Soon, as the canal swings east, The Cloud begins to shadow your progress. You leave the canal just before it crosses what the map calls an 'aqueduct'. However, there's no long series of arches, just an embankment with one short span where the canal crosses over the River Dane. The walk descends slightly to make the river's acquaintance, albeit briefly, before beginning the climb.

This starts with a steady ascent on a lane then continues more steeply, first through pastures and then on rougher slopes clothed in heather and bilberry. The luxuriant growth almost smothers the contours of the old track that once served the quarry on the north face. From a shelf, which extends below the quarry itself, you climb between the crags. This final phase of the ascent is very steep but brief.

### Views From the Crest

You arrive at the northern end of a rocky spine about 100yds (91m) long; the trig point is at the southern end while the actual highest point is midway along. You can sit on the edge of the crags with your legs dangling as you enjoy the view.

**Walk 7**

Eastward the ground rises again, into the Peak District. The nearer hills are in Staffordshire. So, for that matter, is the eastern slope of The Cloud, though the summit belongs to Cheshire. Further north, the highest ground is in Derbyshire, though Cheshire claims the western foothills, including the sharp peak of Shutlingsloe (► Walk 12).

The western half of the view, which stretches over virtually all of Cheshire, is best appreciated from a short way down the descent. Lower down there's a fine pine plantation and some younger woodland. Finally the route drops down the flank of the ridge and into the edge of Timbersbrook.

### Silk Industry

In the 18th century Timbersbrook was a centre of the silk industry. The buildings were later taken over by a bleaching and dyeing company. At its height the works employed up to 230 people. It finally closed in 1961 and the mill and chimney were demolished in 1970s.

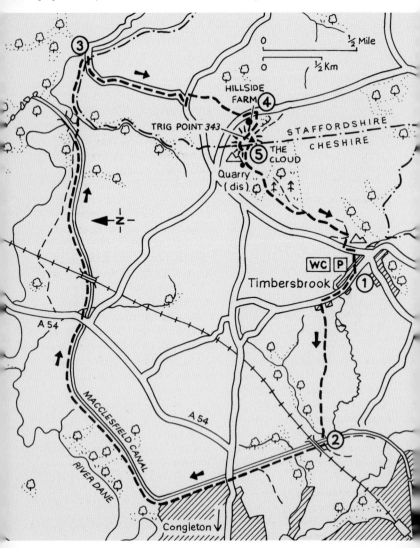

## Walk 7 Directions

① From the car park, turn right down the road for 500yds (457m). Just past some houses, go left over a stile and down a track. After 600yds (549m) go right over another stile. Follow a trodden line to cross a stream in a dip. Continue diagonally across another meadow. A short embankment leads to a canal bridge.

② Cross and loop round left, under the bridge and along the tow path. Follow this for 3¼ miles (5.3km) to bridge 57. Go up the steps and over the bridge. A vague track bears left then swings right through gorse along the edge of a hollow. Descend to a stile under a sycamore then down an often muddy slope to a footbridge. Cross another stile, go down to the **River Dane** and step round a tree on its edge. Turn right up the edge of a field.

### WHERE TO EAT AND DRINK
There's no pub in Timbersbrook, but the **Waggon and Horses Inn** is less than a mile (1.6km) down the Rainow Hill road. It serves Robinson's beer alongside good value food. It's quite small inside but there's a beer garden behind, backing on to open fields.

③ Go over a stile to a road. Turn right and climb steadily. As it levels out, go left on a narrower lane. Opposite a house cross a stile on the right, then up fields over a series of stiles, bearing slightly left. Join a lane and go left, past **Hillside Farm**, then right, up a track to a stile.

④ There's a National Trust sign, 'The Cloud'. The path is narrow but clear, directly uphill then slanting right. It passes below some crags then levels out and dips slightly to the start of a broad shelf. A path now goes straight up the hillside, through the highest band of crags, to the summit ridge. The trig point is about 100yds (91m) to the left.

### WHILE YOU'RE THERE
The main radio telescope at **Jodrell Bank** is usually conspicuous in the view from The Cloud. The 250ft (76m) dish, completed in 1957, has played a hugely important part both in the tracking of space probes and in the understanding of the history of the universe. The story of the observatory and of the science to which it has contributed enormously is told in a fascinating visitor centre.

⑤ Retrace this short section of summit ridge then follow the edge down, gently descending and swinging slowly left. Lower down the path runs through pine plantations. Below a gap in a wall, a broader track runs through more open woods. As the track starts to curve left, a clear path continues straight ahead. Stick to the crest of the ridge until you rejoin the gravel track near a sharp bend. Just below the bend there's a footpath sign and a steeply descending line of steps. Turn left on the road, into the edge of **Timbersbrook**. Just after the first house on the right go through a gap in the fence, down a few more steps and across a field with picnic tables. At its far end is the car park.

### WHAT TO LOOK FOR
Meadows in the early part of the walk support such **flowers** as ragged robin, selfheal and meadow buttercup, as well as a variety of grasses. The canal tow path is lined with typical waterside plants, one of the loveliest of which is meadowsweet. It's a member of the rose family – not immediately obvious from the masses of tiny creamy-white flowers.

**Walk 8**

# Sandstone Trails and Hidden Crags of Frodsham Hill

*A short and simple walk on the crest and along the flanks of a prominent red sandstone escarpment.*

| | |
|---|---|
| •DISTANCE• | 3 miles (4.8km) |
| •MINIMUM TIME• | 1hr |
| •ASCENT / GRADIENT• | 375ft (114m) ▲▲▲ |
| •LEVEL OF DIFFICULTY• | 👫 👫 👫 |
| •PATHS• | Clear woodland paths, golf course, 4 stiles |
| •LANDSCAPE• | Largely wooded steep slopes and gentler crest with a few open sections |
| •SUGGESTED MAP• | aqua3 OS Explorer 267 Northwich & Delamere Forest |
| •START / FINISH• | Grid reference: SJ 518766 |
| •DOG FRIENDLINESS• | Can run free in woodland sections |
| •PARKING• | Small car park on Beacon Hill, near Mersey View |
| •PUBLIC TOILETS• | In Frodsham village and at Castle Park |

## BACKGROUND TO THE WALK

Frodsham is at the northern end of the Sandstone Trail, a 34-mile (55km) walk. The sandstone ridge that bounds the western edge of the Cheshire Plain is not completely continuous but does dominate the lowlands along much of its length. In a few places it breaks out into real crags, notably at Beeston (near Walk 4) and at Frodsham and Helsby.

### Bare and Bold

Frodsham and Helsby hills form a classic case of what geographers call an escarpment. The strata slope gently down to the south east: this is the dip slope, while the craggy fronts facing the Mersey are the scarp. The crags of Frodsham mostly lurk among the trees and are only seen at close quarters. Helsby is a different story: its crags are higher and stand out bare and bold in a profile recognisable from many miles away.

Both sets of crags were once popular with climbers. Until the 1970s Helsby was regarded as a crag of considerable significance. Today, however, it is out of favour. One reason, at least according to climbing legend, is the development of a fertiliser factory just downwind! In the case of the smaller crags of Frodsham, once favoured for short practice climbs, the development of artificial climbing walls is probably the most significant factor in their fall from popularity.

### In Trust

On Woodhouse Hill, near the southern end of the circuit, there was once a hill fort, probably dating back to the Iron Age. It can be hard to discern the remains now, though it's easier if you go in the winter when they're less obscured by vegetation. This area, and the adjoining Snidley Moor Wood, are now owned and managed by the Woodland Trust, a worthy organisation dedicated to preserving and improving woodlands for quiet recreation, access and conservation.

**Walk 8**

**Jacob's Ladder**

After a steep descent the walk returns along the base of the scarp then climbs up through Dunsdale Hollow to the base of the crags. Here you can return to the crest by a flight of steps, though there's an alternative for the adventurous in the steep scramble known to generations of Frodsham people as Jacob's Ladder. Footholds carved in the rock are now so worn that their artificial origin is less obvious. The first 20ft (6m) are the most awkward.

Above this the path passes more small crags, some of them eroded into convoluted shapes, before emerging into the open at Mersey View, crowned by the village war memorial. As the name suggests, the grand curve of the Mersey is unmistakable. Hugging the nearer shore is the Manchester Ship Canal, joined almost directly below by the Weaver Navigation. Beyond it you can pick out Liverpool's airport and the city's two cathedrals.

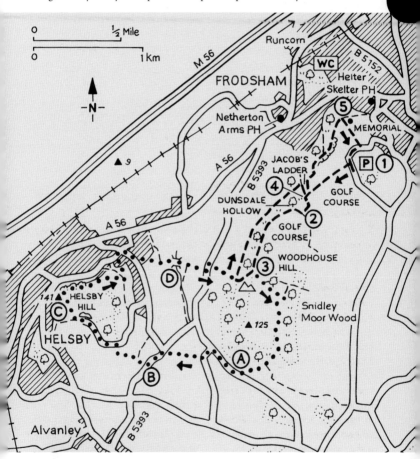

## Walk 8 Directions

① Go right along the lane for 100yds (91m), then left down a sunken footpath and over a stile on to a golf course. The path is much older than the golf course and officially walkers have priority, but don't take it for granted! Head straight across and you'll arrive at the 17th tee, where there's an arrow on a post. Drop down slightly to the right, crossing a sandy patch, to a

**Walk 8**

footpath in the trees right of the green below. Bear left at a sign for Woodhouse Hill, down a few steps. Keep to the left, passing above crags, then go down steps into **Dunsdale Hollow**.

② Go left, rising gently, below more crags. Go past a stile on the left then up scratched steps on the corner of the rocks ahead. Follow a level path through trees, near the edge of the golf course. Soon after this ends, the path rises slightly and passes a bench. After another 20yds (18m), the path forks. Keep straight on along the level path, soon passing a Woodland Trust sign, to a wider clearing with a signpost on the left near the corner of a field beyond.

---

**WHERE TO EAT AND DRINK** ⓘ
The **Helter Skelter**, on Church Street in Frodsham, is named after the centrepiece of the fairground which used to stand on the hilltop, where there's now an ugly modern hotel. The food and beer are excellent and the atmosphere warm and friendly. An alternative, with outdoor seating and a no-smoking area, is the **Netherton Arms** on the A56 between Frodsham and Helsby.

---

③ Just before the corner of the field there's a break in a very overgrown old wall on the right, from which a narrow path slants steeply down the slope. There's some bare rock and it can be slippery when wet, so it needs a little care. Near the bottom it turns directly downhill to the bottom corner of the wood. Go

right along the base of the hill. After 800yds (732m) the path twists and descends a little into the base of Dunsdale Hollow. Cross this and go up the other side alongside a stone wall and up a flight of steps. Go right on a sandy track, climbing steadily then passing below a steep rock face.

---

**WHILE YOU'RE THERE** ⓘ
You can hardly ignore the chemical industry, especially from Mersey View, and you can find out a lot more about it at the **Chemical Industry Museum** in Halton, near Widnes. Just across the unmistakable Runcorn Bridge is **Norton Priory**, dating back to the 12th century. Lewis Carroll, author of *Alice's Adventures in Wonderland* (1865), was vicar of nearby Daresbury.

---

④ Go left up steps, briefly rejoining the outward route. **Jacob's Ladder** is just to the left here, up the right-hand edge of the crags. When you reach the top, bear left with a signpost for Mersey View, and follow a sandy track, with occasional Sandstone Trail markers, along the brink of the steeper slope. This passes below some small steep crags before emerging near the summit obelisk.

⑤ Turn right just before the memorial on a clear footpath, aiming for telecommunications towers ahead. Go through the ornate iron gates on to the lane and turn right, back to the car park at the start of the walk.

---

**WHAT TO LOOK FOR** ⓘ
**New red sandstone** is about 200 million years old – which is fairly 'new' in geological terms! It's a relatively soft rock, as you can see from the worn footholds of Jacob's Ladder. Curious knobbly shapes in some of the crags often result from wind erosion. Despite strenuous efforts at clearance, **rhododendrons** remain abundant in parts of the woods. Originating in the Himalayas, they are very hardy plants which frequently crowd out native species.

# High Rocks of Helsby

*The bare crags of Helsby Hill are the highlight of this longer walk.*
**See map and information panel for Walk 8**

| | |
|---|---|
| •DISTANCE• | 6 miles (9.7km) |
| •MINIMUM TIME• | 2hrs |
| •ASCENT / GRADIENT• | 855ft (261m) ▲▲▲ |
| •LEVEL OF DIFFICULTY• | 🚶🚶 🚶 |

## Walk 9 Directions (Walk 8 option)

At the clearing (Point ③), go left along the edge of the wood. At the end turn right on a wider, sandy track and follow it gently downhill. It's distinctly sunken in places. Eventually it levels out and comes out to a lane (Point Ⓐ).

Go right for 350yds (320m) then turn left on narrow **Burrows Lane**. As it bends left there's a gate on the right with a footpath sign. Follow field edges to a footbridge and then a kissing gate. Continue, now on the other side of the hedge, to a lane. Go left for 200yds (183m) then right (Point Ⓑ) on a green track.

Follow this until it becomes overgrown. Go over a stile on the right and up a short slope, then round the edge of the field. About 50yds (46m) beyond the next stile, go right up a fenced path to a lane. Go left and follow the lane to its end then bear left on a track. When it splits, go right and up to the trig point on **Helsby Hill** (Point Ⓒ).

Though expansive, the view is a mixed bag. Liverpool lies beyond the sweep of the Mersey, but chemical plants, refineries and the M56 clamour for attention. Further away leftwards are the Clwydian Hills. On a clear day, reputedly, you can see Snowdon. The crags below were once very popular with climbers, but have fallen from favour. Apparently the nearby fertiliser plant has made them green and slimy!

Go right, across the top of a gully splitting the crags, then steadily down through oak woods. Where the path forks keep right and descend to a stile, then go left down a track signposted 'Old Chester Road'. Lower down the track squeezes between gardens to the street. Go right, then right again on **Bates Lane** to a footpath on the left, signed 'Woodhouses, Frodsham'. Follow this, then cross the corner of a field to a stile.

A few paces right is another hedged path. From its end, cross a field and join an old stony track by a ford and footbridge (Point Ⓓ). Go right. The track becomes surfaced. At a T-junction go left 30yds (27m) then right up the drive to **The Holt** (a house). Just before the gate of the house go left through a kissing gate into the corner of the wood. Walk 8 comes in from above. Go left along the base of the hill.

# Northwich Canals

*A gentle walk taking in a stunning piece of Victorian engineering.*

| | |
|---|---|
| **·DISTANCE·** | 5½ miles (8.8km) |
| **·MINIMUM TIME·** | 1hr 45min |
| **·ASCENT / GRADIENT·** | 100ft (30m) ▲ ▲ ▲ |
| **·LEVEL OF DIFFICULTY·** | 🚶 🚶 🚶 |
| **·PATHS·** | Woodland paths, surfaced tracks and tow paths, 2 stiles |
| **·LANDSCAPE·** | Woodland banks, fields, occasional industrial backdrop |
| **·SUGGESTED MAP·** | aqua3 OS Explorer 267 Northwich & Delamere Forest |
| **·START / FINISH·** | Grid reference: SJ 653764 |
| **·DOG FRIENDLINESS·** | Sensible dogs can be off leads on most of walk |
| **·PARKING·** | At Marbury Country Park, open till 8PM summer, 5PM winter |
| **·PUBLIC TOILETS·** | Close to car park (► walk directions) |

## Walk 10 **Directions**

The presence of natural brine springs, exploited since Roman times, and of rock salt, mined since the 17th century, made Northwich the cradle of Britain's chemical industry. Directly or indirectly, this has influenced all the landscapes on this walk. The Marbury Estate, the basis of today's country park, was partly built on wealth from salt and was later owned by ICI, who used the hall (which is now demolished) for staff housing.

From the left-hand corner of the car park (as seen when you enter) a gap leads you to an information shelter. Go left up the track alongside an avenue of lime trees. The track bends right, past toilets and the ranger office. Follow it to its end then continue on a footpath to the shores of **Budworth Mere** and turn right.

Skirt a small 'harbour', which gives a good view across the mere to the sailing club and Great Budworth church, then leave the waterside and go left on a broader path. Follow the main path to a fork and bear left, following a sign 'Anderton Nature Park and canal'. Along here there's a wonderful sculpture (Phil Bews, 2001) made from a fallen tree, as well as lots of rhododendrons. A more open area is good for bluebells in season.

When you come suddenly to the banks of the canal, follow the path round to the right, looping away then back left to a stile that leads into **Marbury Lane**. Go left over the bridge and continue down the lane to a dip, where there's a gate on the right with a sign 'Nature Park and Boat Lift'. Go down a short track then detour 50yds (46m) right and up steps to a bird hide, which gives a view over Haydn Pool. Return to the last junction and continue round to the right.

The Anderton Nature Park was once an industrial site and a variety of waste products – such as salt, lime and ash – create conditions which now allow a tremendous

Walk 10

variety of plants to flourish. There's a Wildflower Trail and some of its markers provide useful landmarks for us.

The path first follows a reed-filled inlet then crosses a bridge. The first marker is **No 6**, highlighting ramsons and butterbur, well-suited to this riverside habitat. Ramsons is better known as wild garlic and its aroma is very noticeable in spring and summer.

---

**WHERE TO EAT AND DRINK** ⓘ
The **Stanley Arms**, just up the lane from the bridge above the boat lift, has a beer garden alongside the canal, as well as extensive play facilities. It's also a starting point for boat trips. With a wide-ranging menu too, almost the only thing you can say against it is that it gets a bit busy.

---

Take the left path here then, at the next junction, slant back right past **marker No 4**. Go left along the main track and over a bridge to a crossroads, by marker No 3. Orchids grow in the open shade here. Go right, passing **marker No 9**. At the next junction keep right again, out into an open area, then left at a fingerpost. At a T-junction go right and out into the open, close to the **River Weaver**, with a good view of the soda works.

Just beyond **marker No 2**, descend some steps, go past the rifle range, then take a green path away from the river to the dragonfly pond – and another great wooden sculpture. The water here is too salty for fish and frogs, which makes it relatively safe for the larvae of damselflies and dragonflies. If nothing else, throughout the warmer months you should see lots of electric blue damselflies, flying low over the water.

Return to the riverbank and continue towards the **Anderton Lift**, now rising ahead. Climb steps alongside the overspill channel, signed 'car park and canal basin'. At the top, turn left along the tow path as far as the bridge over the branch to the lift. Then retrace your steps and continue along the tow path, passing the **Anderton Marina**.

Follow the tow path for another ½ mile (800m) to the first overbridge after the marina. Go up steps and over the bridge. After 20yds (18m) cross a stile on the right. Keep left on muddy paths, soon meeting a wider gravel path. Go left, looping round into a narrow strip of woodland between the lane and a large pasture.

At a junction with a track, go right signed 'car park' then, after 100yds (91m), go left through a kissing gate. Go straight ahead, back to the avenue of lime trees, bear left and left again past the information shelter into the car park.

---

**WHILE YOU'RE THERE** ⓘ
The **Anderton Lift**, the first of its kind in the world, represents an ingenious solution to the problem of the 50ft (15m) height difference between the Weaver Navigation below and the Trent and Mersey Canal above. Most of the work was done by allowing extra water into the upper trough, making it heavier than the lower one. With the decline of canal traffic, it became underused and neglected, finally closing in 1983. Restoration started in 1998 and it's now fully operational once again. A new visitor centre alongside the lift is due for completion in Spring 2003. Boat trips, several times daily, give you the opportunity to experience the lift for yourself.

# Wizardly Wanderings at Alderley Edge

*Layers of history and legend surrounding this famous Cheshire landmark make this short walk a rich mixture.*

| | |
|---|---|
| •DISTANCE• | 3 miles (4.8km) |
| •MINIMUM TIME• | 1hr |
| •ASCENT / GRADIENT• | 445ft (136m) ▲▲ ▲▲ ▲ |
| •LEVEL OF DIFFICULTY• | 🚶🚶 🚶🚶 🚶 |
| •PATHS• | Woodland tracks and paths, some field paths, 7 stiles |
| •LANDSCAPE• | Woodland, scattered sandstone crags, some farmland |
| •SUGGESTED MAP• | aqua3 OS Explorer 268 Wilmslow, Macclesfield & Congleton |
| •START / FINISH• | Grid reference: SJ 860772 |
| •DOG FRIENDLINESS• | On lead on farmland and always under close control |
| •PARKING• | Large National Trust car park off B5087 |
| •PUBLIC TOILETS• | At car park |

## BACKGROUND TO THE WALK

There's a lot to take in at Alderley Edge, on the ground, under the ground and even – many believe – in other dimensions entirely.

### Ancient Mines and Legends

As long as 4,000 years ago, there was mining activity here, using tools of wood and stone. Mining went on through Roman times but reached its greatest intensity in the 19th century. Copper and lead were the main products, though various other ores were also worked.

Alderley Edge is as rich in legend as it is in minerals. In fact it is probably true that it is rich in legend because of its long history of exploitation. Old shafts and levels or overgrown heaps of spoil can mystify later generations and inspire speculation. Also, working underground, especially in the fickle light of tallow candles or primitive lamps, seems to stimulate the imagination. Waves of immigration, such as those of Cornish miners, import new layers of legend, too.

### A Hidden Cave

The most famous legend of the area is alluded to in the names of the Wizard Inn and Wizard's Well, both passed on this walk. Hidden somewhere on the Edge is a cave, guarded by a wizard, in which an army of men and horses sleeps, ready to emerge and save the country when the need is dire. No one has found this cave (though it must be a big one) but you can see the wizard, or at least an effigy, carved in the rocks above the Wizard's Well.

### Air of Mystery

This story, and the general air of mystery which often pervades the edge, especially on a misty day with few people about, have inspired many of the books of local author Alan Garner, of which the best known is *The Weirdstone of Brisingamen* (1960).

Walk 11

The walk itself is largely through woodland. In fact the wooded aspect of Alderley Edge is relatively recent. The demand for fuel, building timber and pit props, ensured that the area was cleared of its trees from the Bronze Age onwards. The local landowner, Lord Stanley, began extensive plantings in the mid-18th century and today the National Trust manage the woodlands carefully. Although the Edge is elevated above the surrounding countryside, its wooded nature means that distant views are rarely unobstructed. From the crest of Castle Rock there is a broad window to the north, towards Manchester with the hills of Lancashire beyond, while at Stormy Point the view opens to the east, towards the Peak District.

There are exceptions to the woodland rule. Behind Sand Hills, in the earlier part of the walk, there are damp areas with many orchids, and pools fringed by yellow iris and reed mace (the tall club-headed reed often wrongly called the bulrush). Nearing the end, there's some open farmland.

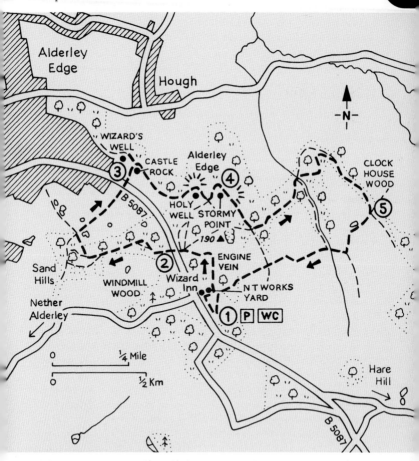

## Walk 11 Directions

① From the large National Trust car park, just off the B5087, walk towards the tea room and information room. Go right on a wide track past the National Trust works yard, then left. Cross an open area past **Engine Vein**. At a crossroads of paths turn left and come out by **Beacon Lodge**.

**Walk 11**

② Go straight across the road into **Windmill Wood**. Follow a gently descending track to a clearing, bear left and continue descending. About 140yds (128m) beyond a National Trust sign, in more open terrain now, with bare sand hills ahead of you, bear right across the grass to a crossroads with a field ahead. Turn right, skirting around some damp ground and then a pool. Just before another open field, go right, along the edge of the wood. Continue in a narrow strip of trees, with fields either side. Cross the road again and follow a track to the bare crest of **Castle Rock**.

---

**WHAT TO LOOK FOR** ⓘ

Signs of **mining activity** can be seen in many places, most noticeably at Engine Vein and Stormy Point. There are deep covered shafts within the open working of Engine Vein. Most of what you see today was excavated in the 18th century, but there is evidence of much earlier working. The exposure of bare rock at Stormy Point is partly due to toxic minerals, though wear and tear by the feet of visitors plays a part too.

---

③ Descend the steps to a level path. Go left 120yds (110m) to **Wizard's Well**. Return to the steps and continue below the crags on a terrace path, then up steps to join a higher path. Go left and almost immediately start descending again, with more steps in places. At the bottom cross a footbridge and climb again, levelling out briefly by the **Holy Well**. A few paces to its left

go up over tree roots to where the path resumes. Climb shallow steps to a wider path, go left then turn right on to the rocky crest of **Stormy Point**.

---

**WHERE TO EAT AND DRINK** ⓘ

The **Wizard tea room**, open 1–5PM weekends and bank holidays, serves great cakes. The adjacent **Wizard Inn** is really a smart restaurant. For normal pub service, including decent beer and a good range of meals, there's the **Royal Oak** on Heyes Lane down in Alderley Edge village.

---

④ Follow the wide level track to a crossroads and go left. Follow signs 'Hare Hill', down a steady descent with a small ravine at the bottom. Turn right and ascend again. Climb steps past tall beech trees, then descend through **Clock House Wood**. Climb again to a National Trust sign and out into the open.

⑤ Go right, over a stile, across the waist of a field to another stile near a pond. Go left along the hedge to a stile hidden in a curve, then up a fenced path. Join a wider track and at the top and go over a stile on the right. Go left over the next stile and up to another stile and grassy track. Cross a gravel track into another narrow fenced path and at its end turn left. Opposite the National Trust works yard you can go left through a gate for a shortcut to the car park or continue straight on to the tea room.

---

**WHILE YOU'RE THERE** ⓘ

There's a working **watermill** at Nether Alderley. The building dates from the 15th century though most of the machinery is more recent. It's also a chance to find out exactly why Millstone Grit is so called. The walled gardens and surrounding park of **Hare Hill**, probably best known for azaleas and rhododendrons, can be reached by a longer walk from Alderley Edge. About 2 miles (3.2km) away, it's fairly well signposted. The gardens are cared for by the National Trust

# Shutlingsloe: the Mini-mountain

*A short but intense walk from enclosed valleys and forest to a stark peak.*

| | |
|---|---|
| •DISTANCE• | 5 miles (8km) |
| •MINIMUM TIME• | 2hrs |
| •ASCENT / GRADIENT• | 1,129ft (344m) ▲▲▲ |
| •LEVEL OF DIFFICULTY• | 𝄃𝄃 𝄃𝄃 𝄃𝄃 |
| •PATHS• | Farm and forest tracks, field paths, lane, moorland, 11 stiles |
| •LANDSCAPE• | Upland pasture, forest, moorland and rocky peak |
| •SUGGESTED MAP• | aqua3 OS Explorer OL24 White Peak |
| •START / FINISH• | Grid reference: SJ 984706 |
| •DOG FRIENDLINESS• | Dogs can run free in forest, sheep elsewhere on route |
| •PARKING• | Small car park at Vicarage Quarry, Wildboarclough (alternative at Clough House, lower down valley) |
| •PUBLIC TOILETS• | At Trentabank in Macclesfield Forest, not far off walk route |

## BACKGROUND TO THE WALK

Shutlingsloe isn't the highest summit in this book, nor the hardest, but it is the one that most closely resembles a child's drawing of a mountain. At 1,660ft (506m) it's also one of the highest points in Cheshire, only exceeded by the hills immediately to its east. Of these Shining Tor, on the Derbyshire border, reaches 1,834ft (559m), but – despite its enticing name – it is a shapeless lump by comparison. Shutlingsloe has a special place among Cheshire hills.

### Macclesfield Forest

A direct approach from Wildboarclough is both steep and short, and doesn't really satisfy. Shutlingsloe deserves better. Devious though it may seem, a loop round through Macclesfield Forest adds substance to the walk and, though still steep in parts, is less drastic than the direct approach.

Macclesfield Forest is the name, not only of a lot of trees, but also of the hamlet that sits in a wrinkle of the hills. Its Forest Chapel dates from 1673 but owes its present appearance to Victorian rebuilding. It was originally a 'chapel of ease' for those who could not regularly make the trek to the parent church at Prestbury. It became an independent church in 1906 and St Saviour's, Wildboarclough, was in turn a subsidiary chapel. The chapel attracts large numbers to its annual rushbearing service, conducted in the churchyard.

Macclesfield Forest (the one with the trees this time) serves a practical purpose as a source of timber, and the reservoirs provide Macclesfield with most of its water, but it is also important for leisure and wildlife. The dark forest floors under the spruce trees are relatively bare, but the trees themselves are a good place to look for the tiny goldcrest. Although it's Britain's smallest bird, its active habits and bright orange cap make it relatively easy to spot. One of our largest birds, the heron, is also well represented, the colony on the shores of Trentabank reservoir being the largest in the Peak District. Stands of tall foxgloves are seen in recently cleared areas; they are among the first plants to colonise disturbed ground.

**Walk 12**

The contrast between the enclosed forest and the exposed moors is intense, whether it's bright sunshine or a stiff breeze (or both) that greets you. The path across the moors is well-marked and, for much of its length, has been surfaced with large gritstone flags, and more recycled stone makes the final steep rise straightforward. There's a view indicator just left of the trig point. There's a steep start – no flags yet – to the descent but then it gradually eases. The waters of Clough Brook once powered a mill, but most of this has now disappeared.

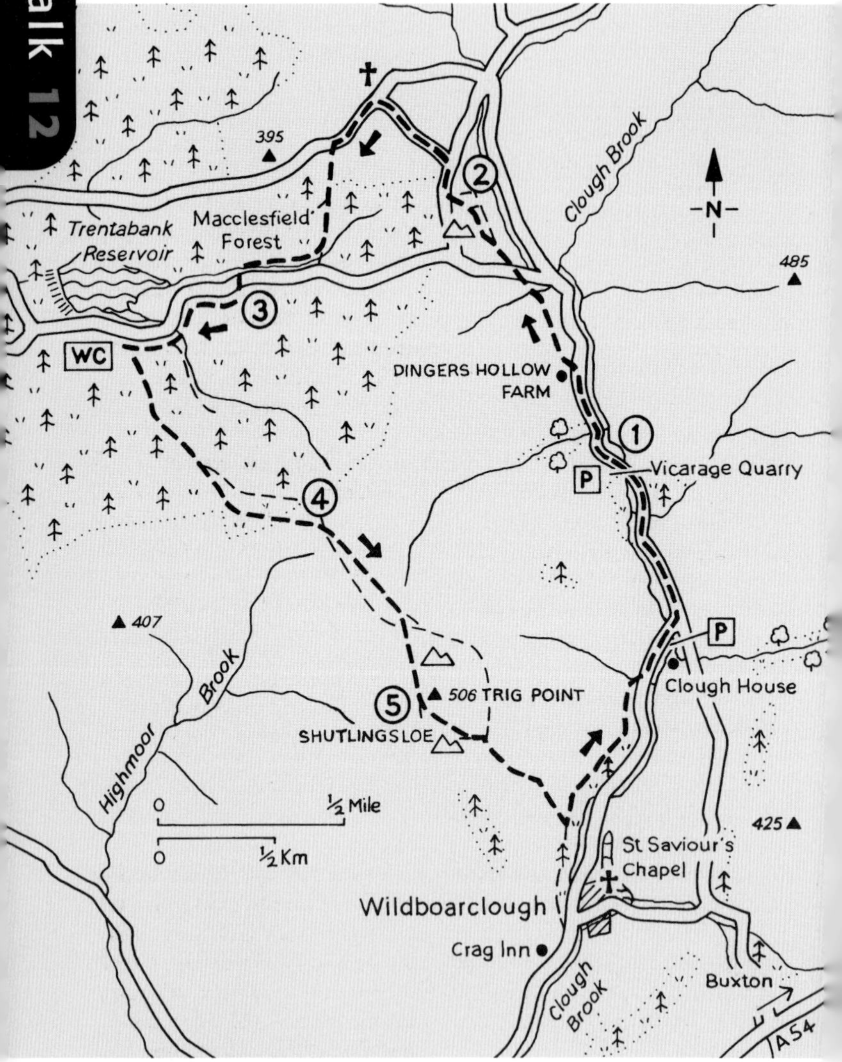

Clough Brook

▲ 395

Trentabank Reservoir

Macclesfield Forest

② 

③

WC

DINGERS HOLLOW FARM

④

① Vicarage Quarry

P

485 ▲

▲ 407

⑤ ▲ 506 TRIG POINT

SHUTLINGSLOE

P

Clough House

425 ▲

–N–

½ Mile

½ Km

Highmoor Brook

St Saviour's Chapel

Wildboarclough

Crag Inn ●

Clough Brook

Buxton

A54

## Walk 12 Directions

① From the car park at **Vicarage Quarry**, turn left up the road, away from Wilboarclough village. Just past **Dingers Hollow Farm**, go over a stile on the left and up to an iron gate. Go right through another gate and follow a green track across the hillside to a third gate. Cross a field near a power line, down to a stream then up left to a stile by a gate. Cross the lane and walk up a few paces to another stile. A narrow path rises gently beyond, but our route rises more steeply, above large oak and ash trees. Continue on this line to a stile into another lane. Go right to a junction.

### WHILE YOU'RE THERE

It's only a few miles over the hill to **Buxton**, one of England's great spa towns, developed as a northern rival to Bath. The Victorian Opera House is not to everyone's taste, but there's much more unanimous approval for the elegant architecture of the 18th-century Crescent, set against fine formal gardens. On the edge of the town you can venture underground at Poole's Cavern.

② Turn left, on a lane signed 'Macc Forest Chapel', over the top and down, past the chapel. Follow the road for another 250yds (229m) to a dip. At the corner of a wood go left on a footpath, straight down the hill. At the bottom, near a small dam, take a newly made permissive footpath on the right, over a small bridge. When a gate blocks the way, drop to the left, down steps to a stile and road.

③ Cross to a gap in the wall almost opposite. The continuation path parallels the road; when it rejoins it by a gate, bear left on a wider path,

### WHAT TO LOOK FOR

**Bilberries** can be found in many places, especially along the verges and the edge of the forest. It's a member of the heather family, though the resemblance is not immediately obvious. Small globular pinkish flowers appear from April to July, followed by the blue-black fruits. These are delicious when ripe, but be warned that they were once also harvested for dyes.

swinging back right. Go up a flight of steps on the left and sharply back left on a path climbing alongside a stone wall. When the gradient eases near a kissing gate, bear left on the more established footpath. When you get to the next junction, after about 300yds (274m), go right, with a sign to Shutlingsloe, and up to a kissing gate.

④ The footpath, partly surfaced here with large gritstone flags, crosses open moorland. At a shoulder the path levels out and Shutlingsloe rears up ahead. Descend slightly, cross duckboards to a stile and then follow the obvious, flagged path alongside the wall. A final steep staircase leads directly to the trig point.

### WHERE TO EAT AND DRINK

The **Crag Inn**, Wildboarclough, provides overshoes – like those used in operating theatres – to cover your muddy boots. It's a thoughtful touch that many more pubs ought to copy, and seems to sum up the welcome. There's sheltered outside seating, while an open fire usually cheers the interior. The menu isn't extensive but everything on it is done well: you get a slice from a real pie, for example, rather than a dish with a disintegrating pastry 'lid'.

⑤ Descend straight ahead, winding down very steeply between several low outcrops. Keep straight on as the gradient begins to ease. After a couple of stiles follow a wall down to a tarmac track. Go right along this to a cattle grid then take another track sharply back to the left. This runs more or less level along the hillside, then a gently descending green track interrupted by a stile and a small stream leads down to the road. Go left up this back to the start.

# Tegg's Nose Meadows

*The set-piece comes early and the rest of the walk unfolds gentler views.*

**Walk 13**

| | |
|---|---|
| •DISTANCE• | 5 miles (8km) |
| •MINIMUM TIME• | 2hrs |
| •ASCENT / GRADIENT• | 1,152ft (351m) ▲▲ ▲ ▲ |
| •LEVEL OF DIFFICULTY• | 🚶 🚶 🚶 |
| •PATHS• | Mostly on tracks and quiet lanes, some field paths, 17 stiles |
| •LANDSCAPE• | Steep green hills and valley slopes are main backdrop |
| •SUGGESTED MAP• | aqua3 OS Explorer OL24 White Peak |
| •START / FINISH• | Grid reference: SJ 950733 |
| •DOG FRIENDLINESS• | Can run free in country park, sheep and traffic elsewhere |
| •PARKING• | Tegg's Nose Country Park, on Buxton Old Road |
| •PUBLIC TOILETS• | At car park |

## BACKGROUND TO THE WALK

The breezy crest of Tegg's Nose, with its interesting quarry remains and fine views, is as far as many visitors get, but a longer walk around the area sets it in context and delivers much greater variety. Although centuries of quarrying have undoubtedly altered the outline of Tegg's Nose, it must always have been a prominent and boldly shaped hill. The beds of massive gritstone that form the summit lie above weaker rocks, which form steep slopes where they're not protected from erosion.

While quarries are a feature of many walks in Cheshire and Lancashire, Tegg's Nose is particularly interesting. Examples of preserved machinery, accompanied by explanatory signs, give an insight into how the stone was worked. The stone-crusher, for instance, could pulverise around 100 tons of stone a day. Imagine the noise and dust. Ear and lung ailments were common and so were injuries and deaths, both from falls and from falling rock. Beyond the quarries the track swings round the end of the hill – the 'Nose' itself. The steep slopes add depths to the view south, down to Langley where streams combine to form the River Bollin and across to Macclesfield Forest and Shutlingsloe (► Walk 12). The descent looks west, over Macclesfield and the Cheshire Plain.

The descent is steep, taking you quickly down into woods. Among the beech and oak you'll also find hornbeam. This is often mistaken for beech but its leaves are longer, more pointed and have serrated edges. After crossing Tegg's Nose Reservoir you start to climb again, in the small valley of Walker Barn Stream. Although much of the ascent is on a tarmac lane, it only serves a handful of farms and is usually quieter than the tracks on Tegg's Nose itself. No cars, very few walkers and a handful of bikes seems to be the order of the day.

Once over the A537 there's a more level interlude. A bend in the track, where Walk 14 parts company, gives a view down into the valley of the River Dean, sheltered by Kerridge Hill. The village of Rainow was once a silk and cotton weaving centre and a staging point on a mediaeval packhorse route conveying salt from the Cheshire mines.

The A537 has to be crossed again but the final stretch is a pleasure, over easy slopes where, in summer, you're likely to find good old-fashioned meadows. High walls, with high stiles, separate them. High walls are usually a sign of abundant stone, often cleared from the fields themselves, rather than quarried at a distance.

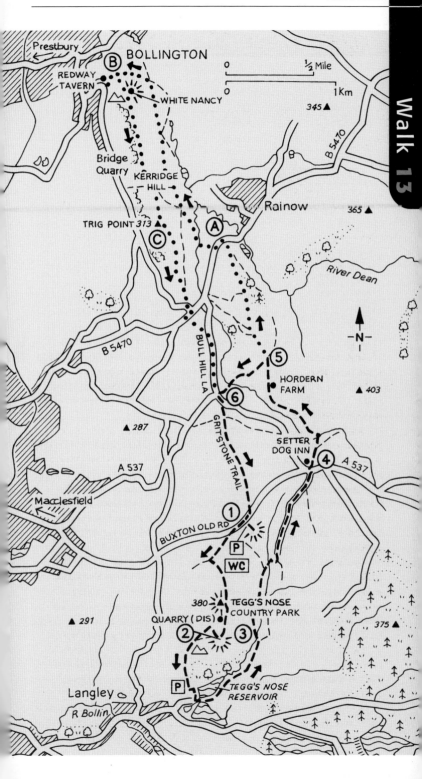

## Walk 13 **Directions**

① From the car park entrance a well-surfaced path, almost level, leads off left. At a gate into the country park, go left up steps, past spoil heaps and then below a quarry face. The path continues past some old machinery and explanatory signs then above the deep bowl of a quarry. Keep left at the next fork, and follow the main track as it swings round the end of hill.

---

**WHILE YOU'RE THERE** ℹ️

Macclesfield was a centre for the silk industry, and preserves much of this history at Paradise Mill and the **Heritage Centre**. The nearby village of Prestbury is centred on a 13th-century church. Just to the south is 15th-century **Gawsworth Hall**, while Marton has a 14th-century half-timbered church, said to be the oldest of its kind in Europe.

---

② Go left over a stile, with a Gritstone Trail sign among others. Descend with stone flags on steeper sections, then mostly on grass and down through a wood to a small car park. Follow the track across the dam of **Tegg's Nose Reservoir** then left up another track alongside the water. At a fork keep left, down to stepping stones.

③ The track climbs then levels out at a stile just above **Clough House**. Drop down to a lane and turn left up it. Follow it up to cross the busy **A537** just above the **Setter Dog Inn**.

④ Almost exactly opposite is a stile and a track down the hill. Where it starts to bend away right, keep straight on down by a stone wall, over the stream and left to an obvious stile. Go left on a pleasant grassy path, just above a collapsed wall, then a level terrace path under beech trees. Keep straight on through the former **Hordern Farm**, and over a rise until the track bends right. Here are two stiles and various signs.

---

**WHERE TO EAT AND DRINK** ℹ️

The **Setter Dog Inn** is well-located, after the main climb on the walk, though the proximity of the busy A537 detracts if you want to sit outside. On the other hand, on a chilly day the roaring fire makes it hard to leave.

---

⑤ Go sharp left over the first (wooden) stile and along the edge of the field. From a second stile, across the field corner, bear right to a stile above a steeper slope. Drop straight down to the stream, angle right then back left above holly trees to another stile. Go straight up past a barn and, from a stile above, bear slightly right and up to **Bull Hill Lane**. Go left to the junction with the **A537**.

⑥ Go left up the main road for about 50yds (46m), cross and go up steps in the wall to a gate and Gritstone Trail sign. Follow the right edge of the field. The line is now almost straight over a series of stiles, with Gritstone Trail signs all the way, first climbing then levelling out and finally descending before meeting **Buxton Old Road**. Go right and down, back to the start.

---

**WHAT TO LOOK FOR** ℹ️

An obvious difference between the Cheshire Plain and the surrounding hills is in the **field boundaries**. Hedgerows are widespread on the plain. In the hills, with ready access to stone, dry-stone walls are the norm. Dry-stone walling is a skilled and time-consuming occupation, but a well-built wall may last for a century or more.

# The Bounding Ridge of White Nancy

*A sharp ridge, dividing the Cheshire Plain and the upland of the Peak District, is the meat of this longer loop.*
**See map and information panel for Walk 13**

| | |
|---|---|
| •DISTANCE• | 8½ miles (13.7km) |
| •MINIMUM TIME• | 3hrs |
| •ASCENT / GRADIENT• | 1,424ft (434m) ▲▲▲ |
| •LEVEL OF DIFFICULTY• | 🚶🚶 🚶🚶 🚶🚶 |

## Walk 14 Directions (Walk 13 option)

At Point ⑤ go over the second (metal) stile and down the field to join a green track between walls. Bear right over another stile and continue following the wall, then descend a narrowing field above trees. Keep on down the spine of the hill to a tarmac lane, Point Ⓐ.

Bear left to the **B5470** and go left until the pavement ends. Cross, descend the track opposite and cross the stream. The path rises again, through ruins and then under a hawthorn hedge, to a stile below an overhanging holly.

Just beyond this the path forks: take the lower one, almost level, for about 750yds (686m) to a fork just beyond a gap in a wall. Keep left and after another 300yds (274m) sidestep right and follow a wire fence. Join a surfaced track and bear left up it. At its highest point, steps climb up to the left, Point Ⓑ. However, for refreshment keep straight on, descending quite steeply, for about 300yds (274m) to

the **Redway Tavern**, subsequently returning to this point. The steps, then a worn path, climb steeply to **White Nancy**. This curious, distinctive bell-shaped structure is normally whitewashed but occasionally decorated for special occasions. Paving around it shows the cardinal points.

Head due south along the ridge, transferring to the other side of the wall, to the trig point on **Kerridge Hill**, Point Ⓒ. The ridge is a sharp dividing line; on the left the Rainow valley and the hills of the Peak District, on the right Macclesfield and the Cheshire Plain. Directly below are fresh quarry workings; compare these raw wounds with those on Tegg's Nose. The path winds through more old workings and descends a quarry incline and runs out to a lane.

Drop down to the main road and go right for around 100yds (91m). Climb steps alongside a shed, before the first house on the opposite side. Go up the right edge of the field, out into **Bull Hill Lane**, and turn right. Walk 13 comes up to the lane just before the junction with the **A537** (Point ⑥).

**Walk 15**

# On the Mersey Beat

*A loop through a great city, starting and finishing on the waterfront.*

| | |
|---|---|
| •DISTANCE• | 3¾ miles (6km) |
| •MINIMUM TIME• | 1hr 30min |
| •ASCENT / GRADIENT• | 180ft (55m) ▲▲▲ |
| •LEVEL OF DIFFICULTY• | 🚶 🚶 🚶 |
| •PATHS• | Streets and pedestrianised waterfront |
| •LANDSCAPE• | Great city with wide river views |
| •SUGGESTED MAP• | aqua3 OS Explorer 275 Liverpool |
| •START / FINISH• | Grid reference: SJ 343896 |
| •DOG FRIENDLINESS• | Dogs may not enjoy this walk, need to be kept on leads |
| •PARKING• | Huge car park for Albert Dock complex |
| •PUBLIC TOILETS• | In Albert Dock complex (and others on route) |

## Walk 15 Directions

Liverpool is ideally suited to exploration on foot. It has the exhilarating sense of space that only harbour cities enjoy, plus a rich history and a unique place in the cultural history of the modern world. Sadly, for many people the name of Liverpool also carries associations with labour problems and riots. Ironically, it was the Toxteth riots of 1981 that sparked a huge effort to revitalise the city, of which the main permanent product was the renaissance of the Albert Dock complex. Dating from 1845, and one of the grandest examples of an enclosed dock anywhere in the world, it's now home to four museums, the Tate Gallery, and a range of shops and bistros.

From the Britannia Pavilion entrance, beside The Beatles Story, walk through to dockside and turn right. Follow it round and cross the **Albert Salthouse Bridge**, then go right, skirting the Salthouse Dock. Cross the main road at the lights and bear left, past the Yellow Submarine and across Chavasse Park, then through Paradise Street Bus Station. Go left to a shopping area then right up **Church Street**.

Opposite Marks and Spencer a short side street leads to the Bluecoat Chambers. Dating from 1717, it's the oldest building, and one of the loveliest, in the city. Return to Church Street, then bear right past the Lyceum Post Office and up long, straight **Bold Street**, once a centre of rope making. At the end cross to St Luke's Church then turn right on **Berry Street**. Bilingual signs are in evidence before the arch leading to Liverpool's Chinatown appears.

---

**WHAT TO LOOK FOR** ⓘ

Liverpool's two **cathedrals** face each other down the length of Hope Street, but they could hardly be more different. The sandstone Anglican Cathedral is the biggest in Britain and took 74 years to complete. The Roman Catholic Cathedral of Christ the King is far more contemporary in appearance yet was completed (in 1967) 11 years earlier.

Opposite the arch, turn left on **Upper Duke Street**, and the Anglican Cathedral looms into view. Turn left into **Rodney Street**, right on **Mount Street** then left on **Hope Street**. Halfway along is the Philharmonic Hall and opposite is the **Philharmonic Hotel**, arguably Britain's grandest pub.

Turn left down **Mount Pleasant**. Bear right at the bottom past the monumental Britannia Adelphi Hotel, then turn right by the Crown Hotel and then up left into the cavernous train shed of **Lime Street Station**. This was the terminus of the world's first passenger railway, linking Liverpool and Manchester. The concourse is worth visiting just to see the clock. Double back to an exit just past the Underground station, out into **Lime Street** and turn right.

If you can see past the traffic, you now get one of the country's great city views, dominated by the massively elegant St George's Hall. If the exterior is impressive, the interior is awesome. Turn left above it, and down **William Brown Street**, past the Walker Art Gallery and Liverpool Museum.

Turn left across the bottom of St John's Gardens. Cross **St John's Lane** and up left then turn right before the Marriott Hotel and under the arch into **Queen Square**. Go under the canopy then right down the steps and left into **Whitechapel**. Follow this down to a pedestrian zone then go right on **Stanley Street**.

Follow the street along to the statue of Eleanor Rigby. Backtrack and turn into **Mathew Street**. This bears slightly right past The Grapes, Cavern Walks, and the Wall of Fame. Beatles' fans will want to spend some time around here.

At the end, turn left then second right into **Lord Street**. This leads to Derby Square, the site of Liverpool Castle. Continue up **Castle Street** towards the Town Hall, a modest building compared to its counterparts in Manchester or even Bolton. Turn left on **Water Street** then right on **Romford Street**. Oriel Chambers, near this junction, was a pioneer of iron-framed construction and a forerunner of skyscrapers the world over.

Turn left on **Chapel Street**, then diagonally left behind St Nicholas Church. Cross **The Strand** and go down the side of the Royal Liver Building to the Pier Head. Along with the Cunard and Port of Liverpool Buildings, the Liver forms the great trinity of Liverpool's seafront. The Liver Birds on top, apparently an improbable cross between a cormorant and an eagle, are 18ft (5.5m) high.

Walk along the **Pier Head** past the Ferry terminal and continue along **Riverside Walk** to return to the start at **Albert Dock**.

# Around Lyme Park Without Prejudice

*A circuit partly within and partly outside the park itself, climbing to an elevated ridge.*

| | |
|---|---|
| •DISTANCE• | 6¼ miles (10.1km) |
| •MINIMUM TIME• | 2hrs 30min |
| •ASCENT / GRADIENT• | 886ft (270m) ▲▲▲ |
| •LEVEL OF DIFFICULTY• | 林 林 林 |
| •PATHS• | Mostly stony tracks with some field paths, 8 stiles |
| •LANDSCAPE• | Woodland, rough pasture and moorland |
| •SUGGESTED MAP• | aqua3 OS Explorer OL1 Dark Peak (southern viewpoint about 100yds (91m) off edge of map) |
| •START / FINISH• | Grid reference: SJ 963824 |
| •DOG FRIENDLINESS• | On lead in deer park, sheep or cattle elsewhere |
| •PARKING• | National Trust car park adjacent to house |
| •PUBLIC TOILETS• | Near tea room, just below car park |

## BACKGROUND TO THE WALK

It's hard to get near Lyme Park without encountering some mention of *Pride and Prejudice*, though the connection is frankly tenuous. In the acclaimed BBC dramatisation of Jane Austen's novel, Lyme Park stood in for Pemberley, Mr Darcy's home. There's no reason to think that Austen herself had Lyme Park in mind. In the novel, Pemberley is in Derbyshire – and was fictional anyway. But never mind; any excuse for a good walk.

### A Wooded Valley

The walk quickly leaves the bustle of the car park for relative tranquillity around Knott – though this can be lively, too, as there's an area where mountain-biking is allowed. The route then descends a wooded valley. The mixture of trees includes Scots pine, sycamore, oak, larch and birch and there are masses of rhododendrons. A good range of woodland birds, from woodpecker to nuthatch, is also present.

Soon the route starts to climb again. Along the first lane are banks of traditional meadow flowers like poppies, ox-eye daisies and cornflowers. Then there's a steady climb through pastureland, punctuated by some self-explanatory place names: Moorside Lane, Keeper's Cottage and Planted Moor. On the last, are several circles of rhododendrons, as obvious and incongruous as any crop circle. Though no one seems to have suggested that these are of extra-terrestrial origin…

### Views From the Crest

It's the sort of climb where a rear-view mirror would be useful as the views expand steadily. Alderley Edge (► Walk 11) stands out, with Manchester Airport slightly further away and the whole conurbation beyond. Reaching the crest, there's a new and very different view ahead. The green little valley of Todd Brook, containing the village of Kettleshulme, seems totally enclosed. It actually drains eastward, towards the higher hills of the Peak District which lie beyond. In reasonable visibility the short out-and-back trip along the near-level ridge is highly recommended to open out the view southward. Kerridge Hill and White Nancy (► Walk 14) are conspicuous and the Cheshire Plain sprawls to the west.

You return along the ridge and continue, still virtually level, towards the isolated Bowstones Farm. Just down to the right are the Bow Stones, two shafts of late Saxon crosses. These may have served as landmarks or boundary stones as well as objects of devotion. The shafts are missing their heads, but these may well be the ones which now reside in the courtyard of Lyme Hall.

You now re-enter Lyme Park and soon descend, with glimpses of the house over the trees. The final section goes through the fallow deer park and then skirts the edge of the gardens, from where you get a classic view of the house reflected by a pool and framed by oak and beech trees.

**Walk 16**

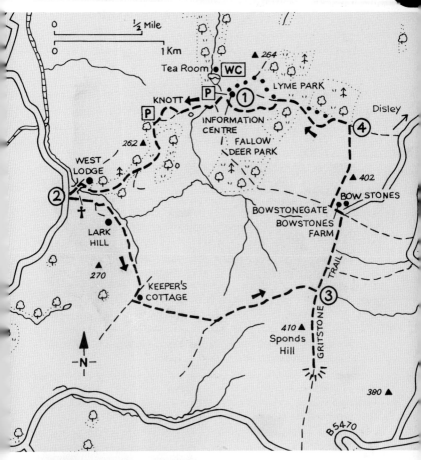

## Walk 16 Directions

① From the **information centre** cross the car park and follow the road left, then swing round to the right. Keep left at a fork then straight on up the low rounded hill of **Knott**. Drop down left to a small car park and through a gate on to a track descending through a wooded valley. Follow this steadily down and out to a lane by **West Lodge**. Go left, over a bridge, and meet a wider road.

② Turn left up the track by a chapel. Where it swings right, for **Lark Hill**, go straight ahead on a level track, then up fields following the **Lyme Park** boundary wall. Swing right to cross a small stream, then up and along the crest of a slight ridge. The path acquires a hard surface where it crosses a level marshy area. Go right on **Moorside Lane**, past **Keeper's Cottage**, then immediately left. Go up alongside a wall to a stile on the crest, then straight down, crossing a green track, to join another track at a gate. Climb again, rejoining the boundary wall. As the slope levels out, the track bears rightwards. One stretch can be boggy, but there's firmer ground further right.

> ### WHILE YOU'RE THERE ⓘ
> It would seem silly to come here and not visit the **house** itself. While the exterior is thoroughly 18th-century and Italianate (by Giacomo Leoni), much of the original Tudor house survives behind the stone façades. But you won't see any interiors from *Pride and Prejudice*: these were filmed at Sudbury Hall in Derbyshire.

③ Follow a good track southward along the crest of the ridge for 750yds (686m) until the ground falls away. Return along the ridge and continue north along the track, towards the very isolated **Bowstones Farm**, just before which the track meets a lane. (The mysterious Bow Stones are just down to the right from here.) From the bend of the lane go left following the Gritstone Trail signs, to cross the boundary wall at

> ### WHERE TO EAT AND DRINK ⓘ
> The **tea room** is a little bare – and noisy when there are school parties in – but the tea's good (National Trust own blend) and they do soup, jacket spuds and bacon butties. There's a wider menu and table service at the **Ale Cellar restaurant** in the courtyard of the house. Don't expect hot food after 2:30PM from either. Otherwise, there are several pubs in the centre of Disley, less than a mile (1.6km) from the park gates, of which the **Rising Sun** is probably the best bet.

**Bowstonegate**. Turn right along the wall and follow it to a corner with a marker stone.

④ Descend the slope alongside a plantation, with rough steps where it's steepest. Lower down the track forks. The main, left, branch gives an easier gradient but they rejoin at the bottom. Go over a tall stile by the corner of the wall, and down a track flanked by a tall deer fence. At a slight bend go left through a gate into the fallow deer park. (This may be closed in the breeding season, in which case continue straight ahead, looping round behind the house back to the car park.) Go over a bridge and follow the edge of the gardens round to the right, then descend shallow steps and through a gate back into the car park.

> ### WHAT TO LOOK FOR ⓘ
> Outside the park, you'll see signposts erected by the Peak District and Northern Counties Footpath Preservation Society, a voluntary body. The main park has **red deer** – Britain's largest native mammal – though with 1,400 acres (567ha) to roam, there's no guarantee they'll cross your path. If you get lucky, you can compare the red deer with the smaller **fallow deer** in their own park.

Walk 17

# A Peak Experience Around Dove Stones

*A magnificent walk along the edge of the moors is the centrepiece of this grand outing.*

| | |
|---|---|
| •DISTANCE• | 8 miles (12.9km) |
| •MINIMUM TIME• | 3hrs |
| •ASCENT / GRADIENT• | 1,296ft (395m) ▲▲▲ |
| •LEVEL OF DIFFICULTY• | 𝄞𝄞 𝄞𝄞 𝄞𝄞 |
| •PATHS• | Mostly on good tracks but with some rocky sections, occasionally very steep, 2 stiles |
| •LANDSCAPE• | Open and exposed moors, with sheltered valleys |
| •SUGGESTED MAP• | aqua3 OS Explorer OL1 Dark Peak |
| •START / FINISH• | Grid reference: SE 013034 |
| •DOG FRIENDLINESS• | Condition of access to moors is dogs must be on leads |
| •PARKING• | Dovestone Reservoir, pay at weekends |
| •PUBLIC TOILETS• | At car park |

## BACKGROUND TO THE WALK

Cheshire's stake in the Peak District National Park is modest, but on this walk you can sample the vast moors so characteristic of the Dark Peak. These are notorious for tough walking over peat and heather, but this is an easy promenade along the edge of the moors; the only hard part is the steep ascent of Birchen Clough.

### Skirting the Reservoirs

It starts easily, alongside a series of reservoirs, allowing you to look up to the crags that necklace the skyline. Dove Stones, directly above the start, has a natural edge as well as a large, long-abandoned quarry. You might also ponder what the King of Tonga was doing at Yeoman Hey Dam in 1981. Above the last of the reservoirs, you follow the Greenfield Brook, climbing gently. The forked tower dubbed the Trinnacle is eye-catching – and you'll get a closer look soon. Don't miss the water-sculpted rocks in the bed of the stream.

### The Dark Peak Moors

Now you make the transition from valley to moor, by the steep ascent of Birchen Clough. The steepest step is alongside a small waterfall and, if it really looks uninviting, backtrack a short way to pick up a path (still steep) which traverses above the obstacle. The easier upper reaches of the Clough, and the flanking slopes leading out on to the moor, are home to substantial numbers of Canada geese.

You reach the edge of the moor close to Raven Stones and soon find yourself looking down on the unmistakable Trinnacle. It's a great foreground for photographs and looks even better with someone standing on the top, but the ascent can only be recommended to experienced scramblers. You have to sidle along an exposed ledge below the lowest top; then it's easier climbing to the middle one but there's a long stride across a deep gap to the highest – and it seems a lot longer coming back!

### Above Dove Stones

The edge is less defined for a time and you cross a vague shoulder past Ashway Cross before clarity is restored. Above Dove Stones the main path keeps back from the edge, but this is magnificently exposed if you don't mind that sort of thing. Just beyond is the isolated tor of Fox Stone. Here a plaque commemorates two Dark Peak climbers who were killed in the Italian Dolomites.

### Rough Shelter

In wild weather, the ruins of Bramley's Cot, once a shooters' hut, provide the best shelter if you need somewhere to take on food and drink. The end wall still stands and you can see the carved sockets where the roof timbers were set. There's still a mile (1.6km) of moor-edge to go before you drop into the valley of the Chew Brook that gives easy walking back to where you began.

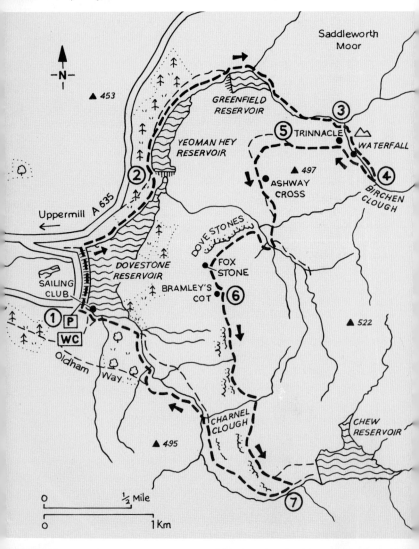

## Walk 17 Directions

① Cross the dam and continue just above the shoreline. Climb up near the end then drop down again to **Yeoman Hey Dam**.

② Follow the left side of the reservoir. At a fork keep to the higher path, rising gently to the next dam. Follow the left side of **Greenfield Reservoir** and then wind on up the narrowing valley. Climb more steeply to more waterworks where the valley forks.

> **WHERE TO EAT AND DRINK** ⓘ
> There's usually a tea/hot dog van at the car park in summer and at weekends. The **Church Inn**, Uppermill (head down the A635, then keep turning right) is a lively place that brews its own beer.

③ Skirt rightwards above a tunnel entrance, then take a rough path up the right branch, **Birchen Clough**. Cross the stream when a steep little crag blocks the way. The path is steep and rough, with one awkward step just below a 20ft (6m) cascade. Above this the clough is shallower and less steep. After some wet patches the clough opens out, with nearly-level ground on the right.

④ Cross the stream and go up right to a marshy terrace. Keep climbing to the right where the slope is less steep. A path materialises just below

> **WHAT TO LOOK FOR** ⓘ
> The Peak District is at the centre of British **rock climbing**. The crags of Ravenstones and Dove Stones are not the most popular in the area, but in good weather you're quite likely to see a few climbers here. The boulders alongside the plantation near the end of the walk are also used for intense micro-climbs.

the plateau edge, rising gently towards the crags. Cross a stile then follow the top of the crags past the **Trinnacle**. After about 440yds (402m) the path forks.

⑤ Go left to a stile, with a cairn just beyond, and a near-level path across the moor. Above a ruin, bear left up a short stony slope, reaching the plateau near **Ashway Cross**. Continue along the edge of the moor, the path keeps generally level, swinging left to cross a stream then back right. Where the path is unclear follow the boundary between peat and rock. The main path keeps a discreet distance from the edge of **Dove Stones**. Beyond the isolated **Fox Stone** the route bears a little left, passing the remains of a stone hut below a crag, **Bramley's Cot**.

> **WHILE YOU'RE THERE** ⓘ
> **Uppermill** is the 'capital' of the Saddleworth district, a cluster of no fewer than 14 villages, many of whose inhabitants still feel their first loyalty is to Yorkshire. The Saddleworth Museum is housed in a former mill alongside the canal at Uppermill.

⑥ Continue along the moor edge, crossing **Charnel Clough**. The path still keeps generally level, swinging left above the Chew valley until the dam of the Chew Reservoir appears ahead. Watch out for the unfenced edge of a small quarry. Skirt round this and down the grass slope beyond to the reservoir road.

⑦ Descend the road until the gradient eases. Just before a gate, drop down left to a ridge. Take the obvious rising path beyond. Slant down right before a plantation, past some boulders. Rejoin the road past the **sailing club** to the car park.

# Douglas Valley Delights

*A gentle yet surprising corner of Lancashire, and it saves the best until last.*

| | |
|---|---|
| •DISTANCE• | 4 miles (6.4km) |
| •MINIMUM TIME• | 1hr 45min |
| •ASCENT / GRADIENT• | 410ft (125m) ▲ ▲ ▲ |
| •LEVEL OF DIFFICULTY• | 🏃 🏃 🏃 |
| •PATHS• | Field paths and canal tow path, 7 stiles |
| •LANDSCAPE• | Open fields, enclosed valley and wooded dell |
| •SUGGESTED MAP• | aqua3 OS Explorer 285 Southport & Chorley |
| •START / FINISH• | Grid reference: SD 517109 |
| •DOG FRIENDLINESS• | Keep dogs on leads until tow path |
| •PARKING• | Large lay-by on A5209 |
| •PUBLIC TOILETS• | None on route |

## BACKGROUND TO THE WALK

They say West Lancashire is flat, and much of it is, but Lancashire is full of surprises. The walk starts with a slight ascent on to High Moor. Not that it is what we would call a moor today: the name dates back to before the Enclosure Acts. As to the 'high' part, that creeps up on you, unsuspected until you start down an enclosed track and then out into an open field. The spire of Parbold church is below you and, to its right, the land falls away to the real lowlands around Ormskirk and stretching away to the sea.

### Napoleonic Fear

Inland you look across the Douglas Valley to the ridge of Ashurst's Beacon which, incidentally, is another grand viewpoint. The beacon was built at the time of the Napoleonic wars, to carry warning of an invasion which many feared was imminent. It was never used.

### Leeds and Liverpool Canal

Now you amble down into the valley. Once this was a major communications corridor. First the river itself was improved for navigation in 1742. Then came the Leeds and Liverpool Canal. This was initiated by an Act of Parliament in 1770, but took 46 years to complete. The cost was, a then colossal, £1.2 million. It remains the longest single canal in Britain. It carried stone from local quarries – much of Wigan is built of Parbold stone – and coal from the Lancashire coalfields.

As one of the later canals to be finished, its heyday was relatively brief. The railway between Wigan and Southport, which runs so closely parallel to the canal through the valley, was opened in the mid-19th century. The canal declined and fell into dereliction but the growth of leisure boating brought a revival.

### Fairy Glen

Having climbed up a little from the canal, and crossed a few fields, you come to the pièce de resistance, Fairy Glen. Its origins are largely natural, rather than supernatural, and there are some traces of small-scale quarrying, but nevertheless there is a kind of magic about the place. Dappled sunlight gilds the rocks and waterfalls. The ground under the trees, depending when you go, may show celandines and wood anemones, wood sorrel, or carpets of bluebells and wild garlic. Between June and September, especially in the lower reaches, there are great drifts of white flowers on loose spikes. This plant could not be more appropriately named for Fairy Glen: it is called enchanter's nightshade. This, incidentally, is a member of the willow-herb family and not related to deadly nightshade. It's over all too soon and the busy road brings a rude awakening, You could always go round again.

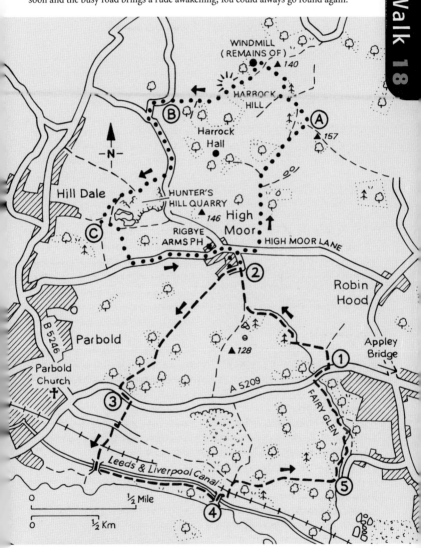

## Walk 18 Directions

① At the end of the lay-by there's a stile into the corner of a field. Go up the side of the field and left

along the top, then into a wood. Cross a small footbridge and continue up the footpath, then alongside a tiny stream. Follow the side of a conifer plantation until it bends away, then bear right to the

**WHILE YOU'RE THERE** ⓘ

Further up the canal, towards Appley Bridge, there's an unusual double set of **locks** – a kind of 'dual carriageway' of the water. **Appley Bridge** itself has a colourful canal basin. **Ashurst's Beacon** offers various short walks and a chance to fill in some of the 'missing' sectors of the view, both east towards high Lancashire and south over Skelmersdale to Liverpool and the Welsh hills.

left-hand side of a clump of trees enclosing a pool. Continue up to the right into an enclosed track below power lines and on up to a junction with a tarmac track.

**WHERE TO EAT AND DRINK** ⓘ

A two-minute detour from the route is all that's needed to find the **Rigbye Arms** – and not even that if you're doing the longer route (▶ Walk 19). There's a range of hand-pulled ales and fine food, including traditional favourites and more innovative dishes. Muddy boots will be most at home in the Fox Hole Bar at the back, and there's outside seating and a play area.

② Go left, then bear left again down an earthy track. (If you're in need of sustenance and want to visit the **Rigbye Arms** first, go right at this point, then left along **High Moor Lane**.) At the end of the earthy track go slightly right, across a field, to the corner of a wood then down its left-hand edge. Keep following this, which eventually becomes a narrow strip of woodland, to a stile in the bottom corner of the field. Follow a footpath down through the wood then up to the **A5209**.

③ Cross the road and go left to a stile where the pavement ends. Go straight down a field and over another stile into a lane. Go right

on this then immediately left down another lane. Cross the railway at a level crossing and continue until you reach a bridge over the canal. Drop down to the tow path and follow it eastwards for about a ½ mile (800m) to the next canal bridge (**No 40**).

④ Cross this bridge and follow an obvious track, taking you back over the railway and up to a gate and stile. Turn right on another track. In places there's a separate footpath alongside, but it's always obvious. Where the track finally parts company go ahead over a stile and along the bottom edge of a field beside an area of new plantings. Cross the next field to a post and then a stile.

⑤ Descend the steep steps down into a wood and bear left into **Fairy Glen**. Cross a footbridge, climb some steps, then go left up a good track. Cross another footbridge below a waterfall and ascend more steps. Keep to the principal footpath, straight on up the glen as it becomes much shallower, until the path crosses a tiny footbridge. Soon after this the footpath leaves the side of the brook and briefly joins a track before it emerges on to the A5209. Cross and go right, back to the lay-by.

**WHAT TO LOOK FOR** ⓘ

A conspicuous plant, of the canal banks in particular, is **Indian** (or **Himalayan**) **balsam**. It has reddish stems and, from July to October, showy white to pink flowers. Even more conspicuous, in a few places, is **giant hogweed**. It can grow anywhere up to 15ft (5m) tall and touching its hairy stems or leaves can lead to a severe skin irritation. Both species were introduced to Britain in the 19th century.

# Over Harrock Hill

*This extended circuit adds variety and expansive views.*
**See map and information panel for Walk 18**

| | |
|---|---|
| •DISTANCE• | 3¼ miles (5.3km) |
| •MINIMUM TIME• | 1hr 30min |
| •ASCENT / GRADIENT• | 560ft (171m) ▲▲▲ |
| •LEVEL OF DIFFICULTY• | 🚶🚶🚶 |

## Walk 19 Directions
## (Walk 18 option)

At the junction with the tarmac track (Point ②) keep straight on to **High Moor Lane**. Turn right then, just past the High Moor restaurant, go left up a concrete track. After 600yds (549m) it curves left.

Keep straight on to a stile, then follow a narrow footpath. Continue along the edge of a wood, Point Ⓐ.

Go left, along the edge of the wood, then straight on and up the edge of another wood. Follow it round right, then go left up the edge of the field and into an area of bracken and birch. Bear left, then left again to the gaunt shell of the windmill on **Harrock Hill**. Its foundations are cut into solid rock. It was active late in the 18th century but fell into disuse by the mid-19th century.

From the ruin slant down left to the wall and follow it to a stile. From the next stile there are wide views over the west Lancashire plains. Follow the left edge of the field down, as closely as gorse permits. Continue on a track past farm buildings, over a stile and down to a lane (Point Ⓑ).

Go left to join a wider road. Ascend this for 400yds (366m) to a footpath sign and stile on the right. The narrow footpath joins a wider track. At a wider, open area keep straight on to follow a narrow path through gorse, close to the fence on the right.

The path skirts the disused **Hunter's Hill Quarry**. The stone from here, known as Harrock Hill Grit, was highly regarded for its resistance to weathering. It was extensively used for construction around Wigan.

Keep right when the path forks then straight on into a sandy track descending past several houses to a junction (Point Ⓒ). Go left, over a stile between boulders and up the paths. Where the gradient eases there's a signpost on the right. Go down the steps then cross the field to a stile just left of a bungalow. Go left up the lane.

At the top, by the **Rigbye Arms**, go right on **High Moor Lane** for about 90yds (82m). Go right down the drive of **Stoney Bank House** then fork right on a grass path behind a hedge. When this meets another track turn right, rejoining Walk 18 just 100yds (91m) from Point ②, where you left it.

# The Paths to Wigan Pier

*A walk to challenge preconceptions, full of wildlife and historical nuances.*

| | |
|---|---|
| •DISTANCE• | 6¾ miles (10.9km) |
| •MINIMUM TIME• | 2hrs 15min |
| •ASCENT / GRADIENT• | 443ft (135m) ▲ ▲ ▲ |
| •LEVEL OF DIFFICULTY• | 🚶🚶 🚶🚶 🚶🚶 |
| •PATHS• | Streets, tow paths and good tracks, can be muddy in parts |
| •LANDSCAPE• | Urban start, semi-urban finish, woodland in between |
| •SUGGESTED MAP• | aqua3 OS Explorer 276 Bolton, Wigan & Warrington |
| •START / FINISH• | Grid reference: SD 576051 |
| •DOG FRIENDLINESS• | Urban start no fun for dogs, but matters improve thereafter, several roads to cross |
| •PARKING• | Main car park for Wigan Pier complex, at Trencherfield Mill |
| •PUBLIC TOILETS• | At start |

## Walk 20 Directions

Many Wigan people still haven't forgiven George Orwell for publishing *The Road to Wigan Pier* in 1937. The book was a firsthand account of working-class life in several areas of England, but because of the title its grim descriptions have been strongly associated with Wigan. And for many in the Wigan area (and elsewhere) life in the 1930s was indeed grim. Much has changed, as you'll see, not least Wigan Pier.

Walk past **Trencherfield Mill**, keeping it to your left, then turn right up the main road. This gives a poor first impression of present-day Wigan but, as you pass under the railway bridge, an unexpectedly elegant street appears. Follow it up to the part-pedestrianised **Market Place** and straight on down.

Just before a dual carriageway go right down setts to **St George's Church**, then left and over a pedestrian crossing. Turn right for 30yds (27m) then down left alongside the **River Douglas**. Follow the path by the river until you reach a turning circle. Cross the left-hand bridge and follow the straight, main track until it becomes rougher. Continue for another 100yds (91m), then descend leftwards with steps, to a bridge over a small stream. Go left on a tarmac track for 50yds (46m) then bear right just before a bridge.

The track descends to the river, rises again then swings back right. Keep left at a fork. A carved boulder indicates the short track into the old quarry called **Devil's Canyon**, now an adventure playground.

> **WHILE YOU'RE THERE** ⓘ
> Attractions at Wigan Pier include the world's largest working mill engine in Trencherfield Mill – an awesome piece of engineering. You can also see working looms in the Machinery Hall. Further round the complex you can visit reconstructions of a coal mine, a Victorian classroom and much more.

Return to the main track and continue another 60yds (55m) then go left up steps. The path leads past former almshouses known as **The Receptacle**, then joins a track across fields. Turn right on a lane (**Hall Lane**) and follow it to **Hall Lane Lodge**. Go left just before the lodge, then fork right to a canal basin. Iron ore and limestone off-loaded here were carried down a tramway where Hall Lane now runs.

---

**WHERE TO EAT AND DRINK** &#9432;
Some people in Wigan clearly have forgiven George Orwell, or the pub in the Wigan Pier complex wouldn't be called the **Orwell**. It's agreeably situated in a grandly-vaulted old warehouse on the canalside, serves a good range of local ales and solid food.

---

Turn right on the canal tow path to an iron bridge (**No 60**). Go right, up steps and down the drive across the old railway, then swing left and down. As it bends back right, go left on a track alongside a brook.

After crossing the stream, go up left to the old railway and turn right. Keep straight on as the path gets narrower (and sometimes muddy), passing under a main road. Follow the virtually straight path through regenerating vegetation. On both sides are housing estates built on former colliery land.

You emerge at a canal basin in the middle of a flight of locks. There are 21 locks in all between Wigan Pier and Top Lock. Though the Leeds and Liverpool Canal reached Wigan in 1781, construction of this flight was one reason it didn't reach Leeds until 1816. The steep mound opposite is known locally as **Rabbit Rocks**. The short climb to the top earns the widest views on the walk,

including Winter Hill eastward and the Peak District due south. The mound is mostly composed of large cylindrical blocks of blast furnace waste – properly known as slag – from the Kirkless Iron and Steel Works, which operated from 1858 to 1931.

The gradual weathering of the slag heap has produced a very alkaline soil, supporting harebells, comfrey and eyebright. The latter has tiny white flowers with yellow hearts. There are also masses of yellow Oxford ragwort, often covered in the tiger-striped caterpillars of the cinnabar moth.

Return to the tow path and follow it down. Cross the road at **Rose Bridge** and continue past **Whalley's Basin**, formerly the junction of a branch canal, now silted up, full of reedmace and popular with anglers.

Cross another road, go under two rail bridges and past the starkly modernist Girobank building. At a canal junction keep to the right branch, cross another road, and return to the tow path.

At **Bottom Lock** your starting point is just to the right, but carry straight on for a proper look at **Wigan Pier**. Go under the next bridge then up and along to a footbridge. Cross this and go left past the **Orwell**. The original pier, a coal loading stage, was in this area. Finally, retrace your steps to **Trencherfield Mill**.

---

**WHAT TO LOOK FOR** &#9432;
Many of the bridges along the route have **cast-iron parapets**. Lord Crawford of Haigh Hall made a great deal of money from iron and seems to have liked to use it ornamentally on the estate.

# Squirrels and Sand at Formby Point

*The effort is minimal and the rewards are great on this exhilarating walk through an area of great significance for wildlife.*

| | |
|---|---|
| **·DISTANCE·** | 3½ miles (5.7km) |
| **·MINIMUM TIME·** | 1hr 30min |
| **·ASCENT / GRADIENT·** | 50ft (15m) |
| **·LEVEL OF DIFFICULTY·** | |
| **·PATHS·** | Well-worn paths through woods and salt marsh, plus long stretch of sand |
| **·LANDSCAPE·** | Pine forest, sand dunes and a vast sweep of beach |
| **·SUGGESTED MAP·** | aqua3 OS Explorer 285 Southport & Chorley |
| **·START / FINISH·** | Grid reference: SD 278082 |
| **·DOG FRIENDLINESS·** | On leads in nature reserve but can run free on beach |
| **·PARKING·** | Either side of access road just beyond kiosk |
| **·PUBLIC TOILETS·** | At start |

## BACKGROUND TO THE WALK

It has to be said that most of the Cheshire and Lancashire coast is fairly urbanised. And as you approach through the town of Formby there's little to suggest that here will be any different. It seems to be somewhere to retire to, or perhaps to commute to Liverpool. This makes Formby Point all the more remarkable.

Tall, shady pine woods form your first impression. They may appear ancient but were actually planted less than 100 years ago, to help stabilise the sand dunes. No one at the time could have suspected that they would become such an important haven for red squirrels.

The dark peaty soils that occur inland of the dunes produce a variety of crops, but a particular local specialty is asparagus. You may still see this growing in the fields that border the reserve early in the walk. On the way out towards the shore you pass a lake, natural in origin, where swans, ducks, coots and moorhens breed.

### Miles of Dunes

The sand dunes at Formby form the largest dune system in England. The line of dunes immediately behind the beach is partly stabilised by the rough-edged marram grass, but high tides and high winds can still change their shape in a matter of hours. The feet of visitors also erode the fragile dunes.

The beach itself is littered with patches of shell debris. Under the sand there are many invertebrates which attract wading birds. One of the easiest to recognise is the oystercatcher, black and white apart from its bright orange eyes, beak and legs. Many other waders and gulls may also be sighted.

As you walk along below the dunes, you will see some darker layers exposed by erosion of the sand. These sediments were formed around 4,000 years ago, when the shape of the coast was somewhat different. In places they have been found to preserve the tracks of animals and birds, so that we know, for instance, that oystercatchers were plentiful then too.

Human footprints have also been found. These suggest that people hunted and fished here, but the most evocative report is of a medley of small prints suggesting children at play.

**A Haven for Wildlife**

From the end of the beach you wind through the sand hills again, past pools where natterjack toads – one of Britain's rarest animals – breed. You'll need to be lucky indeed to see one. Two other rarities that are also found here are great crested newts, around the pools, and sand lizards, in the drier areas.

Finally the walk returns through woods again to the start. Apart from squirrels you may see treecreepers, small brown birds that – as their name suggests – crawl all over the bark of the trees looking for insects.

Walk 21

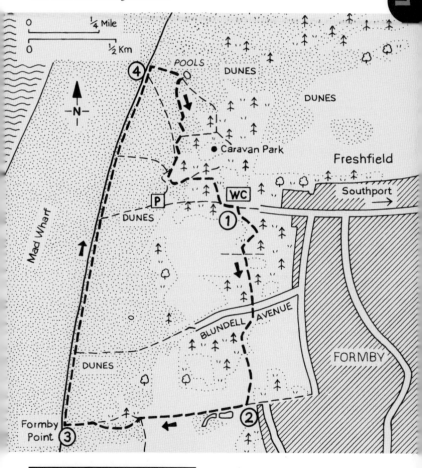

# Walk 21 **Directions**

① Start just left of the large notice board. Follow the '**Squirrel Walk**', with its wooden fencing, to the left and then round to the right. Keep

straight on at a crossroads, where there's a sign for Blundell Avenue. There are many subsidiary paths but the main line runs virtually straight ahead to **Blundell Avenue**. Cross the avenue to a fainter path almost opposite, with a 'No Cycling'

**Walk 21**

sign and traces of bricks in its surface. Follow this, skirting around the edge of a field (brick traces are still a useful guide). Go up a slight rise then across more open sand hills to a line of pines on a rise ahead. Skirt left round a hollow and you'll see some houses ahead.

② Just before reaching the houses turn right on a straight track. This swings left slightly then forks. Go right, down steps, then straight on down the side of a reed-fringed pool. Beyond this keep fairly straight on, towards the sand hills. When you reach them swing left then right, picking up a boardwalk, to skirt the highest dunes and so out to the beach.

### WHILE YOU'RE THERE ⓘ
One way to get to **Southport** would be simply to keep walking along the sands. It's a resort that retains much of the genteel flavour of its Victorian heyday. Amenities are largely as you'd expect, with a boating lake and amusement park, a small zoo and an aviary in Hesketh Park. At low tide the sea can be miles away and instead of windsurfers you'll probably see land yachts.

③ Turn right along the open and virtually level sand. The firmest walking surface is usually some way out from the base of the dunes. Walk parallel to these (heading north) for over 1¼ miles (2km). The shoreline curves very gently to the

### WHERE TO EAT AND DRINK ⓘ
The excellent **Freshfield Hotel** (turn left at the junction about 400yds (366m) east of the level crossing) only serves its good-value food on weekday lunchtimes. This could be a good reason to time your visit accordingly, especially if you're a lover of real ale. At other times, or if you've children in tow, try the **Grapes**, at the other end of Massams Lane.

right but there are few distinctive landmarks apart from signs to various approach paths. It would be all too easy to just keep on going, so watch for a sign for the **Gipsy Wood Path**.

④ A distinct track winds through sand hills then swings more decisively to the right near some pools, where there's a sign board about natterjack toads. Follow the track back into woods and, at a junction, go right. The track curves round between woods and sand hills then joins a wider track by a Sefton Coastal Footpath sign. Go through a patch of willows then bear left to a line of pines on a rise. From these drop down to a broad path with a gravelly surface and follow it left into woods again. Stick to the main path, with timber edgings and white-topped posts, bear right by a large 'xylophone', and it leads quickly back to the start.

### WHAT TO LOOK FOR ⓘ
You'll probably not need to walk too far or look too hard before encountering the **red squirrel** colony. Once familiar throughout England, they have largely been supplanted by grey squirrels, originally from North America, but the wide treeless expanses inland from Formby have helped keep them away here. A much greater rarity, which you'll be lucky to see, is the **natterjack toad**.

# Lancashire's 'Fens' and Martin Mere

*An easy walk on the West Lancashire Plain, under wide skies, around a great bird centre.*

| | |
|---|---|
| •DISTANCE• | 5 miles (8km) |
| •MINIMUM TIME• | 2hrs |
| •ASCENT / GRADIENT• | 50ft (15m) |
| •LEVEL OF DIFFICULTY• | |
| •PATHS• | Canal tow paths, lanes, farm tracks and field paths, 2 stiles |
| •LANDSCAPE• | Flat and open farmland with glimpses of wilder wetland |
| •SUGGESTED MAP• | aqua3 OS Explorer 285 Southport & Chorley |
| •START / FINISH• | Grid reference: SD 423126 |
| •DOG FRIENDLINESS• | On leads across farmland but can be let off on tow path |
| •PARKING• | Several small lay-bys near mid-point of Gorst Lane |
| •PUBLIC TOILETS• | Nothing near by, unless using Martin Mere Visitor Centre |

## BACKGROUND TO THE WALK

The levels of south west Lancashire seem to provide easy travelling: there are miles of canal with no locks and roads and railways with scarcely an incline – and there's easy walking too. However, for most of history these lowlands were an obstacle. Ancient roads and trackways follow the high ground because, until well into the 18th century, this gave easier travelling.

### The Lancashire Mosslands

The Industrial Revolution was closely paralleled by, and to some extent depended on, an agricultural revolution. In many cases the same engineers who built the great canals were also responsible for great drainage schemes. The flat peat Lancashire mosslands were largely transformed into farmland. They fed the growing towns elsewhere in the county with green vegetables, carrots and, above all, potatoes.

Only a few pockets of mossland survive in anything like their original state. Leighton Moss (► Walk 49) is one and the Martin Mere reserve, once a lake, possibly the largest in Lancashire, is another. It's no accident that both are now centres of huge importance for wildlife and especially for birds.

### Wildfowl Reserve

Martin Mere is one of nine centres in the UK run by the Wildfowl and Wetlands Trust, founded by Sir Peter Scott. The reserve itself plays host to a wide variety of resident and migrant birds. Breeding species range from reed and sedge warblers and reed buntings to the spectacular marsh harrier. However, it's the massive flocks of winter visitors that create the most spectacular displays.

The reserve is merely a kind of nucleus and great numbers of geese and swans gather on the fields around, often partly flooded in the winter months. A particular feature is the large number of pink-footed geese – but don't assume that geese with pink feet are necessarily pink-footed geese! They might be greylags – but these are larger and heavier, with longer bills, and may be seen all year round.

Please note that the Wildfowl and Wetlands Trust asks walkers to avoid the paths nearest to the reserve at certain times – specifically from 1 October to 1 April. The reason is that if disturbed the birds may settle further away, on land owned by less sympathetic farmers, and risk being shot. You can't altogether blame the farmers as the birds can virtually strip fields of their growing crops. This request should be heeded and an alternative route is given. You may also want to bear in mind that the ground can be wet at this time of year and you might find the walk more comfortable in wellies.

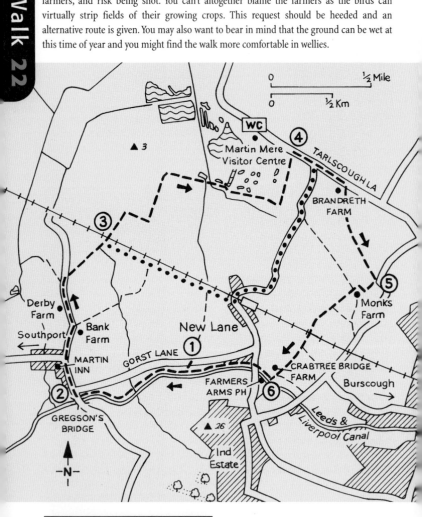

## Walk 22 **Directions**

① Near the mid-point of **Gorst Lane** there's a small timber yard. Follow a short track up through this to meet the canal by a small swing bridge. Go right along the tow path and follow it for about ¾ mile

(1.2km) to **Gregson's Bridge**. Go under the bridge then up to a lane.

② Join a wider road (**Martin Lane**) and follow it away from the canal for about 350yds (320m). At a bend, by the **Martin Inn**, bear right down a narrow lane. Follow this for about 700yds (640m), past the

**WHAT TO LOOK FOR**

The largest birds you'll see and, certainly in terms of weight, the largest wild birds in Britain, are **swans**. There are three species. Mute swans are the most widespread, with curved necks and orange bills. Whooper and Bewick's swans both have yellow bills, but Bewick's are smaller, with thicker necks – altogether more goose-like. Only mute swans breed regularly in Britain.

farm, to a very open section. Opposite some glasshouses there's a footpath sign on the right. Follow the track to the railway line.

③ Cross the line and continue down the track until you come to a green shed. Go right, alongside a drainage ditch, until another ditch appears ahead. Go left alongside this. Continue to a stile by a gate then swing right alongside a reed-lined channel. Follow this over two bridges, the second bridge being close to the corner of the **Martin Mere Reserve**. Continue down a green track, following the edge of the reserve, out to a road (**Tarlscough Lane**).

④ Turn right and follow the road for 500yds (457m). Immediately past **Brandreth Farm** there's a footpath sign. Go down the side of a large shed, go right then left round a pool and on down an obvious track.

⑤ When you reach the end of the track, just before a lane, turn right on a concrete track. Turn right before a house and follow the fence round to the left. Keep almost straight on, past another signpost, and follow a well-trodden footpath through crops towards a couple of trees. These act as direction posts down the field edges to the railway line. Cross and keep straight on, following the slightly raised line of old field boundaries, then join a track to and through **Crabtree Bridge Farm**.

⑥ Swing right on the tow path. It's about 200yds (183m) to the swing bridge by the **Farmers Arms** and another 500yds (457m) to the smaller one above the timber yard. Drop back down through this to **Gorst Lane**.

**WHERE TO EAT AND DRINK**

Two pubs in 5 miles (8km) sounds like a recipe for a jolly walk. Actually the **Farmers Arms** is 50yds (46m) off the direct route of the walk, over the swing bridge. It has both pub and restaurant food including 'create your own pizzas'. Outside tables are a bit close to the car park but have a view of the canal. There's also the **Pinkfoot Pantry** at the Martin Mere Reserve.

**Important Note**

During the main bird migration season (1 October to 1 April) you're requested to avoid the path immediately alongside the reserve. When this applies, an alternative route is as follows: turn right just before the first railway crossing (Point ③). Walk alongside the line to New Lane Station. Turn left up Marsh Moss Lane to the junction with Tarlscough Lane and rejoin the main route.

**WHILE YOU'RE THERE**

Having skirted the **Martin Mere Reserve**, take a look at its 350 acres (142ha). The meres, lined with reeds and trees, are a lot closer to the 'natural' landscape of the area than the bare surrounding farmland. The hides give closer views of many birds – and by paying the admission charge you're supporting the work of the Wildfowl and Wetlands Trust.

**Walk 23**

# A Hidden Gem: Healey Dell

*This is the shortest walk in the book, but it packs a lot in.*

| | |
|---|---|
| •DISTANCE• | 2½ miles (4km) |
| •MINIMUM TIME• | 1hr |
| •ASCENT / GRADIENT• | 640ft (195m) ▲▲ ▲▲ ▲ |
| •LEVEL OF DIFFICULTY• | 林 林 林 |
| •PATHS• | Field paths, old railway line and surfaced tracks, 5 stiles |
| •LANDSCAPE• | Open fields, enclosed and densely wooded valley |
| •SUGGESTED MAP• | aqua3 OS Explorer OL21 South Pennines |
| •START / FINISH• | Grid reference: SD 879155 |
| •DOG FRIENDLINESS• | Can roam free in Healey Dell but not on grazing land above |
| •PARKING• | Parking by Healey Dell Nature Reserve Visitor Centre |
| •PUBLIC TOILETS• | By junction of A671 and B6377, near access road |

## BACKGROUND TO THE WALK

Healey Dell is a gem, and so unexpected. Even from the visitor centre it doesn't look especially promising. In fact it is packed with delights in a small compass. You could spend hours exploring. You'll sample its delights on this walk, but you'll also climb out on to the open slopes above, which give both contrast and context. And although it is a very short walk, its twists and turns make it longer than it looks on the map.

In classic Lancashire fashion, what was once an industrial site is now a haven for wildlife, although the industrial archaeology adds an extra dimension. The fast flowing River Spodden carved the gorge down through the gritstone beds, harder strata creating a number of waterfalls. It also provided a power source for a succession of mills, from early ones grinding corn to later wool and cotton mills.

Near the start of the walk, where the valley is wider, several substantial mill buildings remain. One of these now houses the visitor centre which has permanent exhibitions on the industrial heritage of the reserve. Even in the very tight confines further up, mills were constructed on what must have been very awkward sites, but were unable to compete with larger factories and steam power. The Dell is crossed by the former Lancashire and Yorkshire Railway line. You come down to this line, from the open fields above, close to the site of Broadley Station, where platforms still survive. You follow it through regenerating woodland, feeling quite enclosed, before suddenly bursting out on to the viaduct at treetop height. This impressive eight-arched structure, 100ft (30m) high and 200ft (61m) long, was completed at considerable cost in 1880, but the line was never an economic success.

From its far end you drop down steeply into the shady Dell. Some tumbledown walls remain and a couple of frail-looking arches span the rushing stream. Illustrations from a century ago show these arches still supporting the walls of a two-storey building. Just below, almost directly under the pillars of the viaduct, is an old sluice and the start of the water-cut that fed the great mill pond lower down. You follow the cut down until it disappears into solid rock. This tunnel, probably carved out with nothing more than hand tools, is another example of the extraordinary efforts that were needed to exploit this tricky site. The mill pond itself is now colonised by anglers. As you descend below its retaining wall you get an idea of the depth of water – the head – that it provided to the larger mills just below.

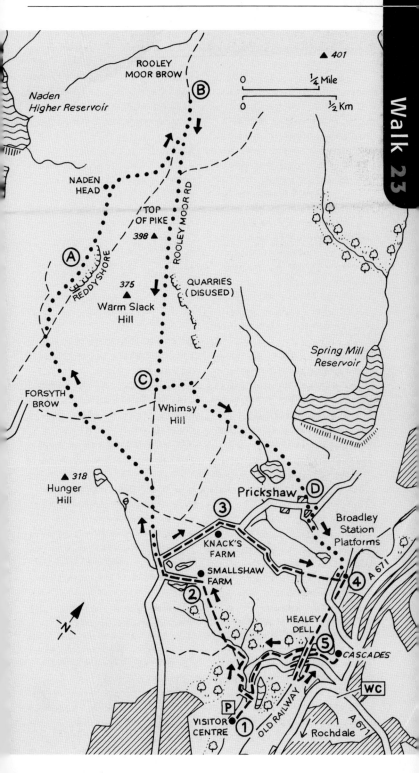

**Walk 23**

## Walk 23 Directions

① With your back to the **visitor centre**, turn left and walk past the first range of buildings. Cross a bridge and turn right. Take the lower path, along the river, past more overgrown ruins. Near a green footbridge go sharp left up the bank then right, along the edge of a clearing, and back into woods. Go left just before a stream on a narrow path, climbing steeply in places. Stone flags give a little help over a wet patch before the path dips to cross the stream. Climb again on the other side and join a broader green track. Where this narrows, continue over a stile and up the edge of a field to **Smallshaw Farm**.

② Go left before the first building then through a gate into the yard. Go left on a track to a road. Go right and up to a bus turning circle. Turn right opposite this along a track. Follow this for about 400yds (366m) to **Knack's Farm**.

### WHILE YOU'RE THERE

Rochdale has a special place in history as the place where the Co-operative Movement, which now has 700 million members worldwide, began in 1844. The **Rochdale Pioneers Museum** is based on the original tiny shop in Toad Lane. Rochdale also has one of the finest Victorian town halls in the region, if not the whole of England.

③ Continue over a cattle grid and down a lane between high banks, then fork right on a track. After a slight dog-leg the track becomes greener. Follow it round left and back right, then over a stile ahead and down a field by a ruined wall. Go over a stile at the bottom, down to a lane and go left a few paces.

④ Go down a ramp and steps to an old railway line. Turn right along it for 500yds (457m) then cross the viaduct high above the **Dell**. Go left down steps to the access lane, down under the viaduct then sharply back right on a broad path. Where this starts to level out there's a stile on the left. But first go a short way upstream, until the path starts to climb again, to see the cascades.

### WHERE TO EAT AND DRINK

The **Oxford** is the first pub you come to on the A671 going towards Rochdale. There's a beer garden at the rear, well insulated from road noise. The beer's well-kept and there's an extensive menu with good fish dishes – check the specials boards around the dining area.

⑤ Return to the stile and cross it. Follow the stone setts (which are often slippery) down to a sharp bend, with more remains just down and right. From the bend a footpath follows the tops of some old walls then curls down steeply to a weir. Step across the water-cut on some stone slabs and follow it down. When it enters a tunnel carved in solid rock, the footpath goes to the right. Almost opposite a tall pillar it swings away from the river and out past a terrace of houses to the lane. Go down this below a tall brick retaining wall and back to the start of the walk.

### WHAT TO LOOK FOR

The steep slopes and, especially, the viaduct, give you an angle on the treetops that you don't often get. This gives great opportunities for close-up views of squirrels, woodpeckers, jays, and many other **woodland species**. The pied flycatcher, which may be seen from April to October, is a distinctive woodland bird, though only breeding males are truly 'pied' – in other words, black and white.

# The Cotton Famine Road

*A longer circuit on to Rooley Moor makes for a dramatic contrast.*
**See map and information panel for Walk 23**

| | |
|---|---|
| •DISTANCE• | 5½ miles (8.8km) |
| •MINIMUM TIME• | 2hrs |
| •ASCENT / GRADIENT• | 1,180ft (360m) ▲▲▲ |
| •LEVEL OF DIFFICULTY• | 👫 👫 👫 |

## Walk 24 Directions (Walk 23 option)

From the turning circle go straight up the hill on a setted track, and then a rougher section. As the gradient eases go left, under pylons, to meet another track. Go left a few strides then right again on a track rising across **Forsyth Brow**. Near the corner of the wall, the track swings right, still climbing easily, then levels off below a steep eroded face at **Reddyshore**, (Point Ⓐ).

The path meets a wall near the ruins of **Naden Head**. Follow the wall up and into a dip, then bear right up an open slope. Keep straight on up to meet the Rooley Moor road again. The well-laid setts date from a relief project during the Cotton Famine of 1862–3, which resulted from supply interruptions during the American Civil War.

Go left for about 300yds (274m) to the ruins at **Rooley Moor Brow** (Point Ⓑ) Near by, until the 1930s, was the Moorcock Inn. Rooley Moor may be deserted today, but within living memory it supported dozens of working quarries, plus several small collieries on the Rossendale side. Skylarks, plentiful on these moors, are among Britain's commonest birds, yet relatively unfamiliar. Small, brown, and inconspicuous, they're usually heard before they're seen, which means that where there's background noise they often go unnoticed.

Backtrack and follow the road down, rising slightly across the shoulder of **Top of Pike**. As the road descends again, there's a splendid view over Rochdale towards the northern hills of the Peak District. The descent becomes steeper, and rougher, eroded by thoughtless motorists although it's not a right of way for vehicles.

Below a short section of restored setts (Point Ⓒ), go left on a track that rises slightly. As it levels and swings further left, cut straight down past old stone pits to another track, part of the old tramway system that served the quarries. It soon swings straight down the slope, continuing alongside a wall. Follow it down between walls, then descend a short flagged section to the restored cottages of **Prickshaw**.

Go left, then right below the lower houses and on down the track. This passes a reservoir, then levels out. Here you go left down a ramp and steps, rejoining Walk 23 at Point ④.

**Walk 25**

# Wayoh and Entwistle

*To moorland, then around several reservoirs that are havens for wildlife.*

| | |
|---|---|
| •DISTANCE• | 4¼ miles (6.8km) |
| •MINIMUM TIME• | 1hrs 30min |
| •ASCENT / GRADIENT• | 295ft (90m) ▲▲▲ |
| •LEVEL OF DIFFICULTY• | 🚶🚶 🚶🚶 🚶🚶 |
| •PATHS• | Mostly on good tracks, 4 stiles |
| •LANDSCAPE• | Rough pasture on edge of moors, wooded watersides |
| •SUGGESTED MAP• | aqua3 OS Explorer 287 West Pennine Moors |
| •START / FINISH• | Grid reference: SD 722172 |
| •DOG FRIENDLINESS• | Reasonable scope for dogs to run free around reservoirs |
| •PARKING• | Batridge Bank car park |
| •PUBLIC TOILETS• | Nearest at Jumbles Country Park, 3 miles (4.8km) away |

## Walk 25 Directions

Tucked into the moors north of Bolton is a string of reservoirs. The oldest, Entwistle, was completed in 1838, originally to serve the string of mills and bleach works in the valley. Today, together with Wayoh (1876), they supply around half of Bolton's water needs. The lower Jumbles Reservoir is a relatively recent addition from 1971. Jumbles is now the centre of a popular country park, while Entwistle and Wayoh, surrounded by mature woodlands, are peaceful places with plentiful wildlife.

From the far end of the car park a footpath rises to the right, with a sign 'Warpers Trail'. Go up steps and

### WHERE TO EAT AND DRINK ⓘ
The **Strawbury Duck** has a great selection of beers, good food including a decent vegetarian choice, outside seating, even a no-smoking room. It was originally the Station Hotel, built around 1900 and extended in 1981 into the much older cottage next door.

over two stiles, cross the access road to a gate then cross a rushy pasture to the road. Go right 100yds (91m) to a track on the left, signed 'Private Road Clough House Farm'.

The track gives easy walking, generally downhill, for almost a mile (1.6km). About 300yds (274m) beyond **Clough House Farm**, go through a gate on the left and down a green track above a little valley. This passes a small mill, the last survivor in the valley.

Just below this, cross the Bolton-to-Blackburn railway at a level crossing. The station has long been closed, though the line remains active. Past the old platforms, you go through the station yard, crossing one remnant of track, then down a lane of fine setts. Where the lane forks go left up a gravel track, to emerge into **Chapeltown High Street** at the side of the **Chetham Arms**. (The Chethams, a Manchester merchant family, once owned nearby Turton Tower). Don't overindulge, as you'll shortly be passing the Police Station.

Walk 25

Turn left. The street is a harmonious collection of fine stone buildings. The name 'Chapeltown' seems a little odd, as the village is actually dominated by the spire of St Anne's Church (which serves the whole Edgworth parish), with not a chapel in sight. Continue through a short section with no pavement then turn right on **Embankment Road**. Go down through the gap, right of a set of gates marked 'Private Drive', and straight down to **Wayoh dam**.

It's worth going a short way out on to the dam to see the elaborate intake on the left and impressive spillway down to the right. Just before the dam a broad track follows the shoreline, mostly through plantations but with plenty of open views. You're encouraged to keep to the track to allow the wild flowers to flourish. There are many birds here too, in the woods and on the water.

After about ¾ mile (1.2km) bear right on a causeway, from where there's a good view of the impressive railway viaduct, often beautifully mirrored in the sheltered waters. At the end of the causeway keep right, still following the shore, swinging round through open plantations. At the end go up slightly then turn right and follow the road across another dam/causeway. Turn left on another good path on the further shore.

The path generally runs a little away from the water to avoid disturbance to the vegetation along the margin. This upper reach of **Wayoh Reservoir** is particularly important in conservation terms, supporting many plants typical of damp areas. One of the more conspicuous is hemp agrimony, which can grow taller than most people in late summer. It has spear shaped, rough-edged leaves and flattened clusters of tiny pink flowers.

Just above the head of the lake cross the river on a footbridge. After a second footbridge, with a 'canal' upstream of it, there are several paths. Go straight ahead, right of a bench. The path then swings left as it starts to climb, past a 'Warpers Trail' marker post. On the way up through the trees, you'll see an iron gantry above the path. This was part of an overhead cableway linking Entwistle Station to a bleach works lower down the valley.

Leave the trees at a stile and go up the field to a gate. Go right up the lane and over the railway bridge. Just beyond are **Entwistle Station** and the **Strawbury Duck**. There's a footpath sign left of the pub. Follow the lane in front of a terrace of railway houses. After passing a few more houses the lane slips down to the dam of **Turton and Entwistle Reservoir**. Cross this to return to the start, though if you've excess energy you could easily do a circuit.

# Ways on Blackstone Edge

*A steady climb to a rocky ridge on the Pennine watershed.*

| | |
|---|---|
| •DISTANCE• | 6½ miles (10.4km) |
| •MINIMUM TIME• | 2hrs 30min |
| •ASCENT / GRADIENT• | 1,066ft (325m) ▲▲▲ |
| •LEVEL OF DIFFICULTY• | 🚶🚶 🚶🚶 🚶🚶 |
| •PATHS• | Field paths, rough tracks and faint paths across open moorland, 2 stiles |
| •LANDSCAPE• | Sheltered valley, rough pasture, bleak and rocky moors |
| •SUGGESTED MAP• | aqua3 OS Explorer OL21 South Pennines |
| •START / FINISH• | Grid reference: SD 939153 |
| •DOG FRIENDLINESS• | Most of walk on grazing land, so dogs under control |
| •PARKING• | Hollingworth Lake Visitor Centre |
| •PUBLIC TOILETS• | At visitor centre |

## BACKGROUND TO THE WALK

Is it or isn't it? Even the experts seem to be divided. It seems fairly clear that there was a Roman road across the Pennines linking Manchester (Mamucium) with what is now Ilkley, in West Yorkshire. And there certainly is an old road over Blackstone Edge Moor. However the stone surface which can still be clearly seen is much more recent and so are the carvings on the Aggin Stone. The route was well-used by packhorse trains and other travellers in medieval times and only faded into relative obscurity with the advent of canals, turnpike roads and railways.

**Old Trading Route**

The best guess of the age of the existing masonry is probably less than 200 years. This may seem a let-down if you're sold on the Roman connection and want to add another nought, but on reflection it's still quite impressive. And those old stones are highly evocative, whether you choose to imagine Roman legionaries tramping up the steep incline, or 15th-century merchants and their trains of horses laden with bales of wool or barrels of salt. Romans or merchants alike would surely have regarded these high, exposed moors as an awkward obstacle to be surmounted, not as an attraction to be sought out. The Pennine Way is an expression of a very different spirit.

The Pennine Way was the first long distance path to be proposed in the UK and the first to be opened: it was officially inaugurated in 1965. It stretches from the Peak District to the Scottish Borders. In fact, it's topped and tailed by pubs: the Nags Head in Edale and the the Border Inn, Kirk Yetholm. In between lie 268 miles (431km) of walking and the stretch over Blackstone Edge is a fair sample.

The huge popularity of the route has created problems with erosion in a number of places. In fact stories about erosion may have contributed to a decrease in the numbers tackling it, though the main factor is the great expansion of a network of other long distance paths, from the South West Coast Path to the West Highland Way. These days far greater concerns about erosion result from the inappropriate and often illegal use of motorbikes and four-wheel drive vehicles.

BLACKSTONE EDGE RES

The rocks of Blackstone Edge stretch for about ½ mile (800m) and have some appeal for rock climbers. The main climbing area is north of the trig point where there are about two dozen routes. Of course this walk is not solely about the ridge. It starts and finishes in softer country dotted with old farms and weavers' cottages. At Syke Farm, near the end, there's another ancient lane. And the hill just above is called Benny Hill, which will amuse some people hugely and others not at all.

# Walk 26 **Directions**

① From the far end of the car park a well-made path runs past picnic tables then crosses and follows a small beck. At a track go left 200yds (183m) then up right with yellow arrows. Zig-zag up the slope then left and down to a stream and footbridge. Where the path forks keep to the lower one, just above

**Walk 26**

### WHERE TO EAT AND DRINK ⓘ

The conveniently-sited **Fisherman's Inn**, a short stroll from the visitor centre, is large and unfortunately smoky, while the outside tables are close to a busy road. A better bet, with good plain food and excellent beer, is the **White House Inn**, high on the moors on the A58. (It can be reached from the walk itself by a detour of about 500yds (457m) each way, following the Pennine Way, from the Aggin Stone.)

the stream. It wriggles through birch woods then up to a wider path and round to **Owlet Hall**.

② Go through the lychgate and left alongside the house to a stile. Cross the stream, and then another stile. Ignore the path on the left and keep right, just above the stream, along a line of thorn trees. Cross a decrepit fence and follow a neglected path alongside a wall. Go up to the trees flanking the drive to **Shore Lane Farm**. Turn left, then left again on a lane.

### WHILE YOU'RE THERE ⓘ

**Hollingworth Lake** was created in 1801 to supply water for the Rochdale Canal and has been a popular spot for local people ever since. There are boating opportunities from launch cruises to kayaking and windsurfing, and coarse fishing, nature trails and a bird hide. It's also reputedly where Captain Webb trained before becoming the first man to swim the Channel in 1875.

③ Just before a road, turn right on a track past some houses. Continue on a narrower but clear path. Meet a farm track just below the **A58**, go right a few paces, then left up the well-worn path 'Roman Road'. Cross a water-cut and keep on climbing. The slope eases near the **Aggin Stone**.

④ Turn right, through a kissing gate and follow a rough path across a rock-strewn moor to the trig point. Follow the main edge south for another 400yds (366m) to a break in the line of rocks.

⑤ Slant down right across rough moor to the old water-cut. Go left alongside this until the path veers off right. It soon rises again, across a shoulder of moor, then levels off by a small cairn. Keep right, along the edge, descend more steeply then swing right, joining an old grooved track. Continue down a green track, past a cairn, then back left descending towards **Dry Mere**.

⑥ Where the ground steepens, just beyond the tarn, the path splits. Take the lower one, towards a pylon. Go straight across a well-used track to another track just below. Go left, fording a small stream, then swing right. Drop down to a shale track in a small valley and go right down it.

⑦ At **Syke farm** join a surfaced lane, which is also ancient. At **Hollingworth Fold**, with its multicoloured signpost, just keep straight on down the lane to join the road along the lake side. The entrance to the **visitor centre** is just across the first embankment.

### WHAT TO LOOK FOR ⓘ

**Peat**, so widespread on the moors of Lancashire and Cheshire, is of relatively recent and partly artificial origin. It is formed by the slow decay of vegetable matter in waterlogged conditions. The conditions for this were created by the clearance of trees in the Bronze Age and by climatic changes. Peat is quickly eroded but slow to regenerate, especially on exposed sites, therefore its wholesale removal for garden use is destructive.

# Rocks and Water at Anglezarke

*A landscape shaped by quarries and reservoirs, full of interest both historical and natural.*

| | |
|---|---|
| •**DISTANCE**• | 7 miles (11.3km) |
| •**MINIMUM TIME**• | 2hrs 30min |
| •**ASCENT / GRADIENT**• | 689ft (210m) ▲ ▲ ▲ |
| •**LEVEL OF DIFFICULTY**• | 👫 👫 👫 |
| •**PATHS**• | Mostly good tracks with some field paths, 20 stiles |
| •**LANDSCAPE**• | Woodland, reservoirs, open valleys and farmland |
| •**SUGGESTED MAP**• | aqua3 OS Explorer 287 West Pennine Moors |
| •**START / FINISH**• | Grid reference: SD 621161 |
| •**DOG FRIENDLINESS**• | Can run free on reservoir tracks, sheep elsewhere |
| •**PARKING**• | Large car park at Anglezarke |
| •**PUBLIC TOILETS**• | Nearest at Rivington (► Walk 30) |

## BACKGROUND TO THE WALK

A string of reservoirs moats the western side of the high moors of Anglezarke and Rivington and quarries scar their flanks. This is not a pristine landscape by any stretch of the imagination, yet today it is seen by many as an oasis of tranquillity close to busy towns and a motorway.

### Reclaimed by Nature

A gentle start just above the shores of Anglezarke Reservoir leads to Lester Mill Quarry, which was worked until the 1930s. The quarry wall is imposing, but somewhat vegetated, and the rock is loose in places. It is much less popular with climbers than Anglezarke Quarry. The name is one reminder that this valley was once a thriving agricultural community. The mill, which served the whole valley, was drowned by the reservoir in 1855. Cheap imports further weakened the rural economy. Today there is only one working farm east of the reservoir.

The route continues through a mix of woodland and pasture to the head of the lake, then heads up the valley below steep, bouldery Stronstrey Bank. There's another quarry high on the right near the end of the bank, seemingly guarded by a number of gaunt, dead trees. Just beyond is another, set further back. Just beyond this an impressive spillway testifies to the potential power of Dean Black Brook.

### A Busy Industrial Village

Now you cross The Goit, a canal that feeds the reservoir, to White Coppice cricket ground. There's a small reservoir just above and you pass others on the way down to the present-day hamlet. These served the mills that flourished here for well over a century. Along with the quarries at Stronstrey Bank these made White Coppice a busy industrial village with a population which may have approached 200. The mill closed in 1914 and little remains today. The railway closed in the late 1950s, the school in 1963 and the church in 1984. This sounds like a story of decline yet today many people would see White Coppice as an idyllic place to live, a fact reflected in the local house prices.

### View to Winter Hill

After White Coppice you climb to Healey Nab. Trees obscure what must have been a fine all-round view from the highest point, but there's a good southward prospect from the large cairn on Grey Heights. Winter Hill is the highest of the moors, unmistakable with its TV towers. The main mast is just over 1,000ft (305m) tall, so you could argue that its tip is the highest point in Lancashire. The string of reservoirs is also well displayed and you get a bird's eye view of Chorley.

The walk finishes across the Anglezarke dam and then, to minimise road walking, makes a short climb to the small Yarrow Reservoir. The final descent gives an opportunity to look into Anglezarke Quarry.

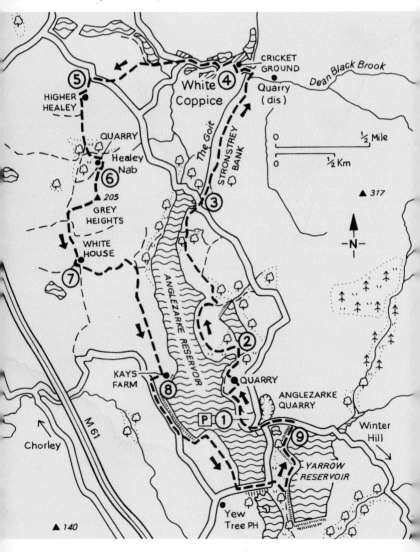

Walk 27

## Walk 27 Directions

① Leave the car park by a kissing gate and follow a track near the water. Fork right, through **Lester Mill Quarry**, then go right, and straight on at the next junction. The track climbs a steep rise.

> **WHERE TO EAT AND DRINK** ⓘ
> The **Yew Tree**, at Lane Ends, 250yds (229m) from the Anglezarke dam, lacks cask beer but has a cosy atmosphere and a choice of bar food or a restaurant menu. Families are welcome and there's outside seating for those with dogs.

② Go through a gap on the left, on a bend. The path traverses a wooded slope. Descend steps, join a wider track and go left. Beyond a stile follow a narrower path until it meets a road.

③ Go left 50yds (46m) to a kissing gate. Follow a track up the valley below **Stronstrey Bank**. Cross a bridge then go through a kissing gate and over another bridge to **White Coppice cricket ground**.

④ Bear left up a lane, then follow tarmac into **White Coppice** hamlet. Cross a bridge by the post-box. Follow a stream then go up left by a reservoir. Bear left to a stile. Cross the next field to its top right corner and go right on a lane. Where it bends right go left up a track.

> **WHAT TO LOOK FOR** ⓘ
> Subtle differences in the nature of the **rock** can be seen in the different quarries. These were significant for the uses to which the stone could be put. Parts of Anglezarke Quarry are 'massive' – there are very few cracks. Some of the rock here is especially pure and was used to line blast furnaces.

⑤ Skirt **Higher Healey**, follow field edges, then angle up left into dark plantations. Fork left just inside, and ascend to an old quarry. Follow its rim for three-quarters of the way round then bear away left through a larch plantation.

⑥ Go left on a clear path then right to the large cairn on **Grey Heights**. Descend slightly right, winding down past a small plantation, and join a wider green track. Bear left over a small rise then follow a track to a lane by **White House farm**.

> **WHILE YOU'RE THERE** ⓘ
> On most days, but especially at weekends, there's a very good chance of seeing rock climbers in **Anglezarke Quarry**. It's one of the most popular venues in Lancashire. A recent guidebook listed 165 routes ranging in severity from Difficult (which isn't) to E6 (which is), and more have been added since.

⑦ Cross a stile on the left, below the farmyard wall, then bear left to the corner of the field. Cross the stile on the left then up the field edge and join a confined path. From a stile on the right follow trees along the field edge to a rough track. Go right and straight on to **Kays Farm**.

⑧ Go right down a track then left on a lane below the reservoir wall. As the lane angles away, go left over a stile then skirt the reservoir until pushed away from the water by a wood. Join the road across the dam. Go through a gap and up a steep track. Go left at the top round **Yarrow Reservoir** to a road.

⑨ Go left, passing the entrance to **Anglezarke Quarry**, to a junction. Go right, and the car park entrance is on the first bend.

# The Deserted Valley of Haslingden Grane

*A walk which, more than most, lays bare the past.*

| | |
|---|---|
| •DISTANCE• | 3½ miles (5.7km) |
| •MINIMUM TIME• | 1hrs 30min |
| •ASCENT / GRADIENT• | 426ft (130m) ▲▲▲ |
| •LEVEL OF DIFFICULTY• | 🚶🚶 🚶🚶 🚶 |
| •PATHS• | Good tracks, a few steep and rough sections, 11 stiles |
| •LANDSCAPE• | Rough pasture and moorland, some woodland |
| •SUGGESTED MAP• | aqua3 OS Explorer 287 West Pennine Moors |
| •START / FINISH• | Grid reference: SD 750231 |
| •DOG FRIENDLINESS• | Mostly grazing land, dogs under control |
| •PARKING• | At Clough Head Information Centre, on A6177 |
| •PUBLIC TOILETS• | In information centre |

## BACKGROUND TO THE WALK

It's hard to believe today, but the Grane Valley was once home to well over 1,000 people. Many houses have vanished entirely, but many more remain, in varying states of decay. It's tempting to assume that it was the flooding of the lower valley that caused its depopulation, but in fact the story is considerably more complicated.

### Growing Population

Settlement began in the area, previously a deer park, in the early part of the 16th century. The population grew over the next two centuries as woods were cleared. However, farming here was nearly always marginal. Most families supplemented their income by handloom weaving. Another widespread source of income was the distilling of illicit whisky. Many of the houses had secret passages or cellars to hide the stills.

As larger mills developed, handloom weaving became less viable. The construction of the Calf Hey Reservoir in the 1850s robbed the struggling community of its best land, but the final nail in the coffin was the crisis which afflicted agriculture in the 1880s, with drastic falls in commodity prices. There's an echo here of the problems which farmers are facing today. Once more, many farmers are searching for supplementary sources of income and in some cases leaving agriculture altogether.

### Abandoned Farms

The crisis of the 1880s led to the abandonment of poorer upland farms in many parts of the region, but the total depopulation of the Grane Valley is one of the most dramatic instances. Even on the opening section of the walk, before crossing the main road, you pass the sites of several farms, a smithy and an inn – though all you're likely to see is a few remnants of wall incorporated into the boundary wall.

As the way swings round the head of the valley it passes several ruins. These stand around 1,000ft (305m) above sea level and it must always have been a somewhat bleak and exposed spot. It's hard to imagine these gaunt shells as they were, with adults working and perhaps children playing. Beyond the ruins the way descends through a conifer plantation but then runs through broadleaved woods, notably a fine stand of beech. These plantings give some idea of how the valley might have looked before it was settled.

As you cross the dam of Calf Hey Reservoir, there are quarries on the skyline both ahead and behind, which also provided employment in the area. Walk 29 takes a closer look at the Musbury quarries. Just before the climb back to the road, the walk passes a graveyard and the sites of both the Methodist chapel and Anglican church. The latter has been re-erected lower down the valley, about ½ mile (800m) beyond the Duke of Wellington pub.

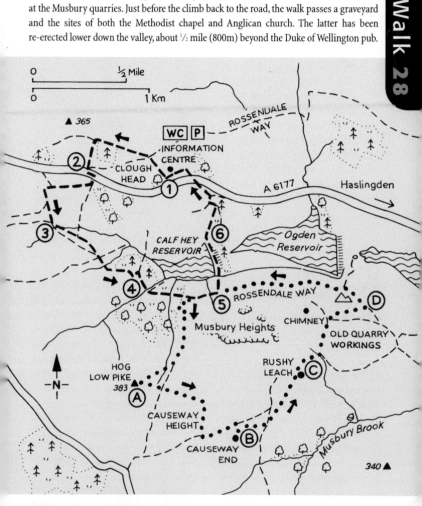

## Walk 28 Directions

① A footpath starts immediately left of the **information centre** building. Go through a small plantation then climb alongside a wall. Cross a stile by a Rossendale Way sign then go immediately left over a stone slab stile and follow an almost level path along a fine wall. After 100yds (91m) past a plantation, go left over a stile by another Rossendale Way sign and down to the road.

② Go left down the road for 90yds (82m), then right on a track, swinging right to pass some ruins. After about 440yds (402m) the

**Walk 28**

track swings left again near some spoil heaps. Keep straight on, past more ruins, then dip into a small valley alongside an old water-cut.

③ Go right 50yds(46m) on a walled track, then left again across a short wet patch. Follow an old walled track past ruined houses and into another small valley, just above extensive ruins. Skirt rightwards round these and descend to the stream then climb up alongside a plantation. Cross into this at a stile. The path starts level but soon begins to descend quite steeply, winding past Rossendale Way signs, to meet a clearer path just before a footbridge at the bottom.

> ### WHILE YOU'RE THERE ℹ
> The **Helmshore Textile Museums** on Holcombe Road (off Grane Road) comprise not one but two working mills. One of them, Higher Mill is still powered by a waterwheel. While you're dipping into the past, you can also travel behind steam on the **East Lancs Railway**, which runs between Rawtenstall and Bury.

④ Cross the bridge and go up steps then across the hillside below a beech wood. Cross another small stream, go up a few paces then go left and follow a generally level path through a pine plantation. Continue along a bilberry-covered hillside above **Calf Hey Reservoir**,

> ### WHERE TO EAT AND DRINK ℹ
> The **Duke of Wellington**, about a mile (1.6km) down the road towards Haslingden, is a spacious establishment with good beer and a standard Brewer's Fayre menu. Children are welcome but dogs will have to remain outside to enjoy the views down the valley. Beer connoisseurs can head to the other side of Haslingden and the **Griffin Inn**, which brews its own.

> ### WHAT TO LOOK FOR ℹ
> Two characteristic birds of grassy moors and upland pasture are the **curlew** and the **lapwing**. Curlews are large brown birds with long down-curved bills. Their long, bubbling call is one of the loveliest and most evocative sounds of the moors. Lapwings are black and white, with a greenish sheen on the back and a small crest. Their *peewit* call gives them their alternative name.

passing a ruin on the left and through a dip containing a small stream. Another 90yds (82m) further, you'll see a large sycamore tree standing on its own.

⑤ Cross a stile just below the tree then descend slightly rightwards to a stile by the dam. Cross it and go up a tarmac path past some valve gear to a gate.

⑥ Go through another gate on the right, then through a gap in the wall and up a path. This runs alongside the road to a car park. Where this path ends there's another up to the left, signed for Clough Head. Go up this, meeting the access road again, then continue up some steps and through a small plantation just below the main road. Go left up the road for 50yds (46m) then cross it by a footpath sign to a kissing gate opposite. A short footpath leads back to the start.

# High on Hog Low Pike

*With views over the Irwell, Darwen and Edgworth valleys.*
**See map and information panel for Walk 28**

| | |
|---|---|
| **•DISTANCE•** | 6¾ miles (10.9km) |
| **•MINIMUM TIME•** | 2hrs 30min |
| **•ASCENT / GRADIENT•** | 820ft (250m) ▲▲▲ |
| **•LEVEL OF DIFFICULTY•** | 🚶 🚶 🚶 |

## Walk 29 Directions (Walk 28 option)

Just before the prominent sycamore at Point ⑤, another path goes sharply back right. Initially almost level, it climbs to cross the fence above the pine plantation. About 50yds (46m) further on, at a crossroads of faint paths, go left and climb alongside the wire fence. Follow it above a steep slope and emerge on to wide moors.

The path forks by a marker post. Go right, across the dip, to a stile then follow the green path across the moor to **Hog Low Pike** (Point Ⓐ). Though not quite the highest point on the walk, it is the most distinct summit.

Backtrack briefly then fork right. Follow a dilapidated wall and wire fence along the broad crest of the moor. The wall fades and then the fence does too. There's a newer fence further right. The path shadows it round a sharp right turn and over the slight rise of **Causeway Height**. Near a stile, and the scar of a recent pipeline, go left on a green path towards a stone wall. Follow it down left, cross at a gap and slant down to the ruins of

**Causeway End** (Point Ⓑ). From in front of the house angle down to a wall, parallel to the previous one.

At its end slant down to another ruin. Follow a narrow level path across the hillside to the ruins of **Rushy Leach**. Around 50yds (46m) further on, by the end of the wall, the path bears right. Follow it to a stile (Point Ⓒ) near the corner of the next wall. Take a level green track, half left, through the old quarry workings and fork left after 50yds (46m).

As the chimney comes into view, there's a signpost. Cross a broader track and take the narrow path slightly right, not the one directly ahead. Skirt the head of a steep 'canyon' to a stile. Descend over a second stile and steeply down to another at the bottom (Point Ⓓ). Turn left along the base of the steep slope to the inclined plane that runs down from the 'canyon'. Both were part of the tramway serving the quarries. There's a short tunnel through the incline, although officially the footpath goes round.

The path runs fairly level and then rises gently, below a steeper slope littered with waste stone. After another stile you rejoin Walk 28 near the large sycamore (Point ⑥).

# Lever Park and Rivington Pike

*A straightforward walk, though steep in places, taking in a superb viewpoint.*

| | |
|---|---|
| •DISTANCE• | 3¾ miles (6km) |
| •MINIMUM TIME• | 1hr 30min |
| •ASCENT / GRADIENT• | 804ft (245m) ▲ ▲▲ ▲▲ |
| •LEVEL OF DIFFICULTY• | 🚶🚶 🚶🚶 🚶🚶 |
| •PATHS• | Mostly clear tracks, well-marked paths |
| •LANDSCAPE• | Managed woodlands, rougher moors and formal gardens |
| •SUGGESTED MAP• | aqua3 OS Explorer 287 West Pennine Moors |
| •START / FINISH• | Grid reference: SD 635128 |
| •DOG FRIENDLINESS• | Can mostly run free, but be careful crossing Rivington Lane and watch out for sheep on moors |
| •PARKING• | At Hall Barn, in Lever Park |
| •PUBLIC TOILETS• | Near car park and just below highest point |

## Walk 30 Directions

William Hesketh Lever, later Lord Leverhulme, left two great monuments in the region. One is Port Sunlight (► Walk 6). The other is Lever Park, which he bought in 1900. Born in Bolton, Lever made a fortune from soap, and spent much of it on philanthropic projects. He intended to present the park to the people of Bolton but legal wranglings resulted in it being gifted to Liverpool instead, though it's the inhabitants of Bolton and Chorley who get the benefit. It can get very busy.

Go round the right side of **Hall Barn** to a red-brick house then down the drive, between ponds, and on down an avenue of beech trees. Keep straight on and cross the busy road to **Great House Barn**. Walk down the track away from it, towards the lake, then go left by some iron railings. Skirt the woodland conservation area and return to the lakeshore. Keep to the lower path, which leads to **The Castle**. This is a replica of Liverpool Castle, not as it appeared in its heyday but in the dilapidated condition in which it appeared around 1900. On Walk 15 you can see where the castle actually stood.

From the castle gate take the long track running straight away. Just before a barrier, with a car park beyond, go left on a short track to the road then straight up the track opposite. This track, sometimes a bit muddy, climbs steadily up the left side of a wood before angling left to join a wide gravel track.

Where this reaches a crest, go sharply back right on a path below a gorse-covered slope. This meets a stony track. Go left through the gate and steadily up the track. Keep on climbing steadily as the gorse thins out and the track doubles back right near a gate (this leads into the

**Terraced Gardens**). The tower on the summit of Rivington Pike soon appears, a lot closer now than it was before.

You go through a gate and rough paths climb up left directly towards the tower but it's a lot less steep to stick to the track then go right by a prominent signpost where the mast on Winter Hill also comes into view. Go slightly downhill to a track on the left just beyond a clump of rhododendrons. Climb this stony track through a couple of curves then finish straight up on eroded paths to the tower.

---

### WHAT TO LOOK FOR

There are still pockets of farmland in Lever Park but before Lever acquired it the area was wholly agricultural. The two outstanding relics of this are **Hall Barn** and **Great House Barn**, both probably 16th century in origin and, though considerably altered, remain fine examples of cruck-framed construction, which uses massive timber trusses. Most of the large trees in the park are around 100 years old.

---

Rivington Pike is 1,198ft (365m) high and was a beacon site known to have been used to warn of the arrival of the Spanish Armada. The tower was built in 1733. It gives a tremendous view over most of Lancashire, extending to Cheshire, Wales and the Lake District. At closer quarters two prominent features are the Reebok Stadium, home of Bolton Wanderers, and the long brick sheds of the Horwich locomotive works.

Descend stony steps in front of the tower then more steps cutting the corner of the track. Then join the track, almost level now, to a gate just above a toilet block. Go right,

above rhododendrons, and descend slightly to the tall, narrow **Dove Cote**. From this, backtrack for about 100yds (91m) to a fork and take the lower track between some stone gateposts. This leads into the **Terraced Gardens**. You can wander and explore pleasantly here for hours and the described route is just one suggestion.

The track leads to a broad level space with the remains of a tile floor, site of a substantial bungalow. Just beyond this, go down steps to a flagged path. Where it splits go left and down more steps and out on to a balcony. Go down and left along the track below, then right through a small arch and down more steps.

Cross a rough track and continue down beside some ruins. Curl down below them and there's a pool on the left, complete with waterfall and grotto. Go down through the rough stone arch and cross a wider path to descend a narrower one slanting to the right. Keep descending in the same general direction, at the same easy gradient, until the track swings left as the slope begins to ease.

Go straight down across a field then through a gate into woodland again. Keep straight on then swing right on a track flanked by a wooden fence. When you reach some buildings pass them on your left-hand side and go down left back to the car park.

---

### WHERE TO EAT AND DRINK

**Great House Barn** has a tea room with a good selection of cakes, but no ale. For this, head up 'over the top', by Winter Hill, to Belmont and the **Black Dog Inn**. Food is good and the Holt's beer well kept. The nearby **Wright's Arms**, up the A675 northwards, is also recommended.

# Darwen Tower and the Freedom of the Moors

*A simple walk, if moderately steep in parts, to a great physical and historical landmark on the moors.*

| | |
|---|---|
| •DISTANCE• | 4 miles (6.4km) |
| •MINIMUM TIME• | 1hr 30min |
| •ASCENT / GRADIENT• | 705ft (215m) ▲▲▲ |
| •LEVEL OF DIFFICULTY• | 🚶🚶 🚶🚶 🚶 |
| •PATHS• | Well-defined tracks throughout, 3 stiles |
| •LANDSCAPE• | Reservoir and wooded surroundings, farmland, open moors |
| •SUGGESTED MAP• | aqua3 OS Explorer 287 West Pennine Moors |
| •START / FINISH• | Grid reference: SD 665215 |
| •DOG FRIENDLINESS• | Dogs can run free on tracks, watch for sheep on moor |
| •PARKING• | Car park near Royal Arms |
| •PUBLIC TOILETS• | At car park |

## BACKGROUND TO THE WALK

The 'right to roam' may be still in the process of being established over most of England and Wales, but has been enjoyed on the Darwen Moors for over a century, and Darwen Tower stands in commemoration. After a long struggle, spearheaded by the Ashton family, rights of access over the moors were transferred to Darwen Corporation in 1896. A large procession of local people climbed on to the moor in celebration.

### The Right to Roam

It's worth remembering that in this, as in most other cases, what was really happening was the re-establishment of rights of access that had existed for centuries. Local people would cross the moors on their way to work in the mills and in the small collieries that existed here. The erosion of these rights in favour of 'sporting' interests caused much resentment and was not forgotten. Free access to these moors today is a right, but should also be considered both a privilege and a responsibility.

### Pleasant Stages

The opening stages of the walk are a pleasant preamble, through the woods around Upper Roddlesworth Reservoir and over a shoulder by some old tracks to Earnsdale Reservoir. Here you are just above Sunnyhurst Wood, Darwen's main park, which provide a direct link from the town on to the moors. Above the reservoirs you climb in stages. After the old quarry you begin the final, longest stage, on a corner of the moors overlooking the town.

### India Mill

The dominant feature, without question, is India Mill dating from the 1860s. The chimney is 302ft (92m) high and its style is not Indian but Italianate. The mill closed in 1991 but now houses new light industry and office space, and there are plans for retail and leisure developments in the subsidiary buildings.

**Darwen Tower**

And so to Darwen Tower. Construction began in 1897, the year after the achievement of access, which also happened to be the Diamond Jubilee of Queen Victoria. The building was opened in 1898. There are 65 wide stone steps, and then 16 iron ones leading to the small glasshouse on the top. The tower did fall into some decay during the middle of the 20th century but was thoroughly restored, with funds from a public appeal, in the 1970s.

Naturally the view is extensive, especially in the northern half. Some of it has changed totally since the tower was built; the new industrial areas alongside the M65 above Blackburn are the most obvious example. But the skylines of Bowland and Pendle are the same. The descent takes you past some old mine workings and a waterworks channel. Just before the end, the row of houses (Hollinshead Terrace) was built as workers' accommodation for a nearby mill that no longer exists.

**Walk 31**

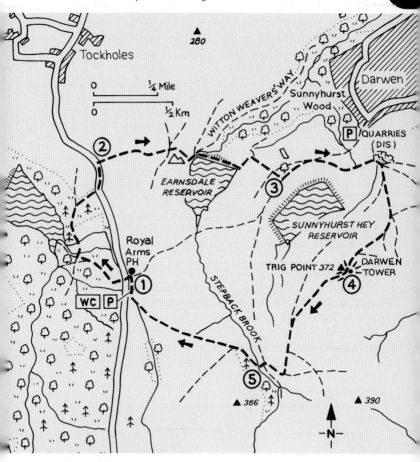

# Walk 31 Directions

① From the car park cross a bus turning area and then the road. Go through some gates and reach a

footpath sign in 30yds (27m). Go right, following the sign for 'Woods and Water Trail'. The path descends steadily to a crossroads. Turn right here on a broad path – still the 'Woods and Water Trail' – then after

**Walk 31**

200yds (183m) go right at a fork on a gently rising path. Gradually curve to the right and climb a little more steeply, with open fields on the left, out to the road. Go left for 200yds (183m).

② Go right up a walled track, part of the Witton Weavers' Way. Go straight on at a crossroads then descend steeply, with a section of old paving, towards **Earnsdale Reservoir**. Cross the dam and swing left at its end then follow the lane up right until it swings left once more, over a cattle grid. Go straight up the steep grass slope ahead, skirting a fenced area with regenerating trees.

> **WHERE TO EAT AND DRINK** ⓘ
> The Royal Arms has an old-fashioned feel inside, with its several small rooms, though in a welcome modern development one is no smoking. The menu is also fairly traditional but still provides a reasonable choice. The garden is a sun trap and has a play area.

③ Go left on a track then, just above a house, bear right up a concrete track. At a gap in the aluminium barrier bear left on a level path towards an old quarry. As this is reached, go up right on a stony track then keep left where it forks. A gate on the left, flanked by fine flagstones, gives a good view of the town of Darwen, dominated by the India Mill chimney. Continue

> **WHAT TO LOOK FOR** ⓘ
> You can look, with care, for old **coal mine shafts** on the moor, in the area where you begin to descend. Usually there's little left to see but a conical pit, with scattered spoil heaps near by forming good markers, but one or two still have open shafts. The deepest of the shafts went down around 200ft (61m).

> **WHILE YOU'RE THERE** ⓘ
> **Tockholes** village, which lies below the main road, is best explored on foot as its streets are narrow in places. There are several fine 17th-century houses, a church and a chapel (and the site of a second). The village school, dating from 1854, has an external pulpit allowing open-air preaching.

up the main track for another 100yds (91m). As the gradient eases and the tower comes into view bear right, past a marker stone on which there's a likeness of the tower, and straight up to the real thing.

④ From the tower bear left past the trig point and along a broad path above the steeper slope that falls to **Sunnyhurst Hey Reservoir**. The path swings left past a bench. Go over a stile on the right overlooking the valley of **Stepback Brook** and down a zig-zag path. Don't cross the next stile but go back left, towards the stream, then over a stile at the bottom. Go left on a track to cross the stream.

⑤ The track swings back right and up through a wood. As it levels out pass to the right of a pair of gates and continue down towards a row of houses. A lane just left of these leads to the road. Go back past the bus turning area to the car park.

Walk 32

# Weaving Ways Around Wycoller and Trawden

*A moderate walk around an upland district steeped in the history of Lancashire, Yorkshire and the textile industry.*

| | |
|---|---|
| •DISTANCE• | 5¼ miles (8.4km) |
| •MINIMUM TIME• | 2hrs |
| •ASCENT / GRADIENT• | 538ft (165m) ▲▲▲ |
| •LEVEL OF DIFFICULTY• | 🚶 🚶 🚶 |
| •PATHS• | Field paths, some rough tracks and quiet lanes, 19 stiles |
| •LANDSCAPE• | Upland pastures, moorland and wooded valley |
| •SUGGESTED MAP• | aqua3 OS Explorer OL21 South Pennines |
| •START / FINISH• | Grid reference: SD 926395 |
| •DOG FRIENDLINESS• | Mostly on grazing land, dogs must be closely controlled |
| •PARKING• | Car park just above Wycoller village (no general access for vehicles to village itself) |
| •PUBLIC TOILETS• | In Wycoller village |

## BACKGROUND TO THE WALK

Everyone associates the Brontës with Yorkshire, but they had strong Lancashire connections too. As children the sisters lived in the north of the county, attending school at Cowan Bridge, only later moving to Haworth, where they wrote their famous books. Haworth is only 9 miles (14.5km) from Wycoller and today you can walk the distance on the Brontë Way.

### Handloom Weavers
Another hint of Yorkshire is the tradition of weaving wool, rather than the cotton usually associated with Lancashire. Trawden had several mills. Wycoller was a community of handloom weavers but as the Industrial Revolution developed they were unable to compete with the growth of larger, powered mills and the village became an isolated backwater.

### Sheep and Cattle
Naturally sheep farming is important here, especially on the higher ground, but the area has a long tradition of cattle rearing too. The distinctive walls of large upright slabs that are seen in places are known as vaccary walls – a vaccary being a cattle farm.

### Quiet First Half
The first half of the walk crosses these pastures, though you'll see more sheep than cattle today. For much of the way you climb gently, with wide views towards Pendle and the Yorkshire Dales, finally emerging on to the open moors. The route now follows an old trackway along the edge of the moor before swinging back down into Turnhole Clough. The path skirts above the woods before dropping into them and crossing the beck. Just below you meet the main Wycoller Beck. About 300yds (274m) below the confluence is the Clam

Bridge, believed to be more than 1,000 years old and made of a single massive slab of gritstone. At least, it was a single slab until 1989, when an exceptionally heavy flood swept the bridge away. It was repaired and replaced, but damaged again the following year. Though the repair has been skilfully done, you can clearly see where the slab was broken.

### Wycoller Hamlet

Following the stream, you soon come into Wycoller hamlet. Despite its simple construction of stone slabs, the clapper bridge is a relatively recent affair, at most only 200 years old. The packhorse bridge is certainly more ancient, possibly over 700 years old. The low parapets, which sometimes alarm nervous parents (though usually not their children), are an essential feature for a packhorse bridge as the animals would be heavily burdened with huge bales of wool.

### Broken Up

Near by stand the ruins of Wycoller Hall. Originally built in the 16th century, the Hall was considerably enlarged in the 18th century by Henry Cunliffe. Unfortunately the lavish works left him heavily in debt and after his death, in 1818, the estate was broken up. It's thought that the Hall was largely derelict by the time the Brontë sisters knew about it and that it inspired Ferndean Manor in Charlotte's *Jane Eyre* (1847).

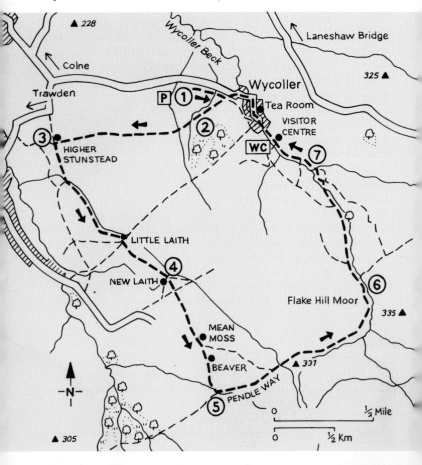

## Walk 32 Directions

① At the top of the car park are a notice-board and a sign 'Wycoller 500m'. Follow the footpath indicated, just above the road, until it joins it on a bend. Cross a stile on the right and slant right across the field to another stile, then up to a gate and into a garden. Follow the arrow through trees up the left side to another stile.

### WHILE YOU'RE THERE

Apart from a closer look at Wycoller itself, with its impressive new visitor centre, you could take a look at one of the more impressive sections of the **Leeds and Liverpool Canal** at Foulridge, just beyond Colne. Narrowboat cruises are available, some of which venture into the Foulridge Mile Tunnel.

② Bear right, cross a stream, then bear left, up towards a house on the skyline, until a footbridge and stile appear in a dip. Follow the hedge and then a wall in the same line. When it ends at open, rushy pasture bear slightly right (towards Pendle Hill, if clear). Cresting the rise, you'll see a stile and signpost by a corner of walls. The sign for Trawden points too far right. Aim slightly left, between two power line poles and again, once over a rise, you'll see a stile and signpost by the end of a fine wall. Follow the wall and then a walled track to **Higher Stunstead**. Go past the first buildings and into the yard.

### WHERE TO EAT AND DRINK

There's a fine **tea room** in Wycoller itself, with a delightful garden. You can find pubs in Trawden and in Laneshaw Bridge on the A6068, where the **Emmot Arms** has a particularly good reputation for both food and beer.

③ Go left up a walled track to a cattle grid then ahead to a stile and follow the course of a stream up to **Little Laith**. Continue to pass the house on your left then go straight ahead, along field edges, to a large barn on the skyline by **New Laith**. Follow arrows round the farm.

④ Continue virtually straight ahead to a stile by a gate and over more stiles to **Mean Moss**. Go a few paces left up a track then follow the wall on the right and more stiles to **Beaver**. Go slightly right down a field to a stile near the corner then up by the stream to a track.

⑤ Go left, then keep straight on above the wall following a rougher continuation (Pendle Way sign). When the wall turns sharp left, the track bends more gradually, above a stream, down to another signpost.

### WHAT TO LOOK FOR

Lively waters like those of Wycoller Beck are an ideal habitat for **dippers**. These small birds may often be seen perched on stones. The distinctive bobbing motion, which gives them their name, can make them hard to spot against the flickering background of running water. If you're lucky you may also see them 'flying underwater', as they feed largely on stream beds.

⑥ Go slightly left to a stile by a gate then take the lower path, down towards the stream then up round a wood. From a kissing gate drop down to cross the stream, then follow it down and out to a lane.

⑦ Go left down the lane to the **visitor centre** and **Wycoller** hamlet itself. From here, go left up the lane and join the outward part of the route for the last 350yds (320m) back to the car park.

# Witching Ways of Pendle

*A grand loop around the flanks and subsidiary ridges of Pendle Hill.*

| | |
|---|---|
| •DISTANCE• | 4¾ miles (7.7km) |
| •MINIMUM TIME• | 2hrs |
| •ASCENT / GRADIENT• | 738ft (225m) ▲▲▲ |
| •LEVEL OF DIFFICULTY• | 🚶 🚶 🚶 |
| •PATHS• | Field paths and rough moorland, surfaced track, 10 stiles |
| •LANDSCAPE• | Wooded foothills and moorland slopes |
| •SUGGESTED MAP• | aqua3 OS Explorer OL21 South Pennines or OL41 Forest of Bowland & Ribblesdale |
| •START / FINISH• | Grid reference: SD 823403 |
| •DOG FRIENDLINESS• | Can run free in woodland and enclosed tracks |
| •PARKING• | Public car park in Barley village |
| •PUBLIC TOILETS• | At car park |

## BACKGROUND TO THE WALK

The name Pendle Hill means 'Hill Hill Hill'. The way this came about is typical of the convoluted history behind so many English place names. If you lived below Pendle, you might well call it simply 'the Hill', and early Celtic inhabitants did just that – 'Pen'. Later incomers, not realising this, called it Pendle, meaning 'the hill called Pen'. This meaning too became obscured, and the name was later applied to the whole district.

### The Wild High Moors

Pendle is also closely associated with witches. In 1612 seven women and two men were hanged at Lancaster Castle (▶ Walk 50). Another old woman died in prison before the case had even been tried. All came from the Pendle area. It is a fact that several of the accused confessed, but whether any of them were witches is an almost unanswerable question today. The story is well told in several books, notably Robert Neill's classic novel, *Mist Over Pendle*. First published in 1951, it remains in print and is readily available in the area.

The walk starts easily, on a well-marked and much-trodden route (part of the Pendle Way) through green fields. While this shorter loop avoids the challenge of the steep upper slopes, it does make a fairly level, but moderately rough, traverse along their base, giving a taste of the wilder atmosphere of the high moors. Perhaps you can begin to appreciate how isolated and remote parts of the district may have felt in the 17th century.

### Alice Nutter

From the plantations and reservoirs of Ogden Clough you climb on to a subsidiary ridge, which gives the best views of the walk, then descend to the small village of Newchurch in Pendle. It was new in 1544, anyway! Although no one knows for sure, it is thought that Malkin Tower, where the witches met, was situated near by. On the tower of St Mary's Church is the 'Eye of God', which was supposed to protect the villagers from witchcraft, and in the churchyard there's a 'witch's grave', possibly that of Alice Nutter.

Beyond Newchurch the route follows the continuation of the ridge, looking down on Roughlee, though caravan sites make it hard to visualise the 17th-century landscape.

Roughlee was the home of Alice Nutter, a gentlewoman who was among those hanged at Lancaster. Although poor, old women, especially widows, were most likely to be suspect, no one was exempt from the paranoia of the times. Anyone who kept a dog or cat, for instance, ran the risk of being accused of consorting with a 'familiar spirit'.

Finally the walk follows the banks of bubbling Pendle Water, past cottages and an old mill, back to Barley.

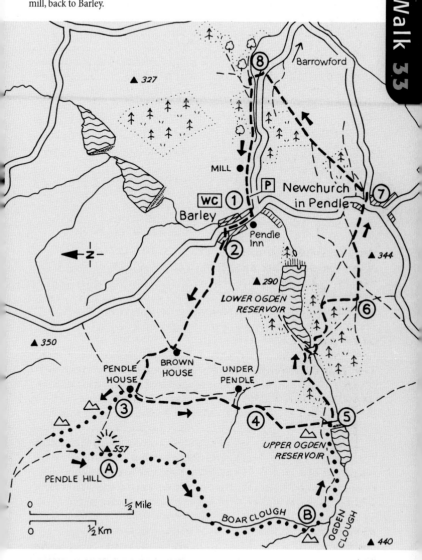

## Walk 33 Directions

① From the toilets follow a path rightwards across the green then over a footbridge. Go right then up the street. Just past **Meadow Bank Farm** go left up a footpath alongside a stream.

② Keep straight on up then cross another footbridge and join a lane.

**Walk 33**

Follow this, with lots of signs, to a kissing gate and a well-marked path that leads up to **Brown House**. Go into the yard, right on a track for 60yds (55m) then left through another kissing gate. Go down and right, then up through new plantings and straight up to a gate left of **Pendle House**.

---

### WHERE TO EAT AND DRINK ⓘ

The **Pendle Inn** dates from the 1930s and the fine, panelled interior is original. There's an open fire, good beer and solid pub food, available all day at weekends. There's also a place to sit outside overlooking the beck, and an extensive play area for children.

---

③ Go left to meet a path just above the wall. After another gate, climb a little, away from the wall. The path runs an undulating course, then dips more definitely and meets the wall again. From a stile (don't cross it) just above **Under Pendle**, bear right and follow the fence. Cross the stream then straight on up a clearer track to rejoin the wall.

---

### WHILE YOU'RE THERE ⓘ

**Pendle Heritage Centre** is 2 miles (3.2km) away, off the B6247 on the outskirts of Barrowford. In a lovingly restored 17th-century house you can find out much more about the story of the Pendle witches, and about the general history of the area. You'll also find lots of 'witch' material and souvenirs at **Witches Galore** in Newchurch.

---

④ Bear right on a trackway climbing alongside an obvious groove. Pass a couple of old wooden gateposts. There's another gate and stile just ahead but instead go left through a gate and straight down by a wall. Cross a track and descend steeply to a gate just below **Upper Ogden Reservoir**.

⑤ Follow the reservoir road until just above **Lower Ogden Reservoir**. Go right over a bridge, down a few steps then round right to a footbridge. Climb steps then go left and climb more steps through a plantation. At its end go up right to the ridge.

⑥ Turn left following a fence then a wall. At a signpost bear right, keeping roughly level until the rooftops of Newchurch appear. Aim for a water trough, then a stile and signpost. Descend a short path to the road.

---

### WHAT TO LOOK FOR ⓘ

The moors of Pendle are largely grassy, less dominated by heather than those of Bowland. There's much greater variety of plants than may initially meet the eye. Low growing **tormentil** has yellow flowers like tiny Maltese crosses: you'll have to get down low to see that it's actually a member of the rose family. The unmistakable fluffy white tufts of cotton grass, also known as **bog cotton**, are a marker for wet ground.

---

⑦ Go down the road opposite, signposted for Roughlee. After about 100yds (91m) cross a stile on the left-hand side and follow a rising footpath. Fork to the left just inside a plantation. At the far end of the plantation keep straight on, gradually converging with the wall on the left-hand side. Follow the wall, changing sides halfway along, to join a sunken track. Cross this and descend to the road.

⑧ Go down the tarmac track opposite, cross the Pendle Water then go left alongside it. Continue on a stonier track past some cottages and an old **mill**. Finally a short path on the right leads back to the car park.

# The Big End of Pendle Hill

*An extended loop and a steep climb to Lancashire's most celebrated summit.*
**See map and information panel for Walk 33**

| | |
|---|---|
| •DISTANCE• | 6 miles (9.7km) |
| •MINIMUM TIME• | 3hrs |
| •ASCENT / GRADIENT• | 1,427ft (435m) ▲▲▲ |
| •LEVEL OF DIFFICULTY• | 🚶🚶 🚶🚶 🚶 |

## Walk 34 **Directions** (Walk 33 option)

Pendle Hill is not the highest hill in Lancashire, but it is the best known, most recognisable and surely the best loved, which ultimately counts for more than mere height. Along with witches, it has more salubrious associations. It was on Pendle that George Fox had a vision that inspired the birth of the Society of Friends (the Quakers).

From the gate by **Pendle House** (Point ③) bear right and up to a kissing gate. Climb straight up on a remade path that soon swings right above the very steep slope by a staircase of large blocks. George Fox 'went on the top of it with much ado, it was so steep,' and you will surely sympathise. As the gradient eases there's a wall and a marker post. Go back left above the slope, joining a well-worn track to the **trig point**, standing on a hump (Point Ⓐ), that may be a Bronze-Age burial mound.

The top is a sprawling plateau, which restricts the views westward, but the eastern half is great. The valley of Pendle Water is directly below. The Yorkshire boundary – and the Pennine Way – run across the first range of hills to the east. Further north is a green expanse, crossed by the Ribble and Aire, and then the Yorkshire Dales National Park. South are Colne, Nelson and Burnley and then more hills, half in Yorkshire, half in Lancashire.

Continue in the same direction, past a huge untidy cairn. At a second enormous cairn the path splits. Keep right, just back from the plateau edge, past occasional smaller cairns, until the path splits again. Take the right branch, which swings further right then runs down past widely-spaced cairns and meets a tiny stream. This soon grows and carves itself a more distinct valley, **Boar Clough**. Cross the stream but keep following it down into **Ogden Clough**.

The descent gets very steep just before the end. Keep right, where it's a little less steep, then go left on a relatively level path. Ford the beck (Point Ⓑ) and go up a little. Contour along the slope then go roughly down to a gate. Follow a narrow clear path above **Upper Ogden Reservoir**, crossing the wall halfway along at a gate. Descend by the dam, joining the reservoir road. Walk 33 comes down from the left just here (Point ⑤).

**Walk 35**

# Rural Revelations in Witton

*Not just a country park but real countryside in the heart of urban Lancashire.*

| | |
|---|---|
| •DISTANCE• | 4½ miles (7.2km) |
| •MINIMUM TIME• | 1hr 30min |
| •ASCENT / GRADIENT• | 558ft (170m) ▲▲ ▲ |
| •LEVEL OF DIFFICULTY• | 🚶 🚶 🚶 |
| •PATHS• | Good paths and tracks, some open fields, 9 stiles |
| •LANDSCAPE• | Woodland, pasture and river bank |
| •SUGGESTED MAP• | aqua3 OS Explorer 287 West Pennine Moors |
| •START / FINISH• | Grid reference: SD 662271 |
| •DOG FRIENDLINESS• | Can run free in country park, but on leads on farmland |
| •PARKING• | Large car park just off A674 |
| •PUBLIC TOILETS• | Adjacent to The Pavilion and at visitor centre |

## Walk 35 Directions

Glance at the map and you may think this is an urban walk, but that's not how it feels. The busy urban backdrop is mostly unseen, though it may come to your ears over the birdsong in Billinge Wood.

Witton Country Park covers 480 acres (194ha) and was formerly the estate surrounding Witton House. The house is now demolished though the stable block remains and is now the visitor centre. The park has a network of paths and nature trails, but this walk ventures out into real, open country.

Walk past the athletics track and **The Pavilion in the Park**, then go left, below the woods, following the

cycle track until it swings left. There's a sculpture – is it a crow or a rook? – perched on a tree on the right. Just before this there's a track on the right. The sign says 'No Horses' but some muddy patches show evidence of mountain bikes.

Follow the track up through a wooded dell. Cross a small bridge over a side stream then up some steps. Go left at the top of these then round to the right, climbing an ever-narrower belt of woodland to a kissing gate at the top, near **Billinge Nook farm**, which has a fine barn.

Go a few paces right on the lane then through a short tunnel and up the track rising to the right, past some magnificent beech trees. Cross one path on a counter-diagonal and continue until ours doubles back – here are two **marker posts**, one bearing No 4.

As the gradient eases, birch and scattered pine rise above the rhododendrons. Stick to the principal path and you soon reach a small open area with a concrete

---

**WHAT TO LOOK FOR** ⓘ

Specimen trees abound on the wooded slopes of Billinge Hill, many still bearing identifying signs, albeit a little faded. Keep an eye out for the the **nuthatch**, sparrow-sized but with a slaty-blue back, which clings to the bark of the trees.

plinth and plaque. This is the summit of **Billinge Hill**. The views are limited to strategic gaps in the trees: south to Darwen Tower and Winter Hill, east to Blackburn cathedral and Pendle Hill, north to Mellor and the Bowland Fells.

---

### WHERE TO EAT AND DRINK  ℹ

The Old Stables Tearoom at Witton Park visitor centre is open from 1PM to 4:45PM (4:30PM in winter), opening at 11AM on Sundays and bank holidays. For pub food try the Clog and Billycock, just 'over the hill' on Billinge End Road.

---

Go down left to a broader path and left along it. The descent becomes steeper, but not excessively, to a T-junction with another path. Go right, uphill for a few yards, then the path trends right before swinging back left to a small parking area. At one corner of this, where wall meets fence, is a stile and a Witton Weavers' Way sign.

Go straight across the field, a little right of the crest, to a stile by a small clump of trees (there are larger patches of trees both to the left and to the right). Just ahead is a knoll above a small old quarry; this is actually a much better viewpoint than Billinge Hill. This area is known locally as **Yellow Hills** because of the stands of gorse. Gorse bears a few flowers throughout the year – hence the old saying, 'when gorse is in bloom, kissing's in season' – but is at its best in spring and early summer.

Carry on down a rough spine, passing walls of single upright stones. **Hoghton Tower** on its wooded hill is dead ahead. Trees shield the depths of Butler Delf, an old quarry (the Butler family owned Pleasington Hall). Go down to the

right, over a stile alongside. A second stile takes you over into the woods and down towards some houses.

Go left a few paces on the track that leads into the quarry, then right at a public footpath sign. Follow this path down and keep straight on, past a Witton Weavers' Way marker post pointing right, over a stile into open fields. Keep straight on in the same line, passing midway between two power line poles, then down to the right edge of the wood ahead.

In the bottom right corner, just right of **Pleasington Old Hall**, there's a stile and 30yds (27m) beyond it a drive. Go right for 200yds (183m) then left along the cycle track, past an ornate milepost. Go past a pool with a view of Pleasington Old Hall, then right down the drive below the cemetery. The gates may be locked to vehicles but pedestrians can still get through. Bear left across football pitches to a metal footbridge, cross it then go left just above the river, dropping down further on to follow the bank through woods.

The next bridge has decorated 'gateposts' and another fancy milepost further on. The mileposts are two of 1,000 placed on the National Cycle Network during Millennium year. Cross this bridge then continue along the river bank and so back to the start.

---

### WHILE YOU'RE THERE  ℹ

Hoghton Tower, glimpsed during the walk, is a late 16th-century house with a fine hilltop setting, open to the public in the summer. Legend relates that it was here, in the banqueting hall, that James I 'knighted' a particularly fine joint of beef, giving rise to the name 'sirloin'.

# Round the Hodder Valley

*A straightforward walk around the delightful heart of the Forest of Bowland.*

| | |
|---|---|
| •DISTANCE• | 7 miles (11.3km) |
| •MINIMUM TIME• | 2hrs 30min |
| •ASCENT / GRADIENT• | 853ft (260m) ▲ ▲ ▲ |
| •LEVEL OF DIFFICULTY• | 👫 👫 👫 |
| •PATHS• | Field paths, farm tracks and quiet lane, 8 stiles |
| •LANDSCAPE• | Pasture and river valley, overlooked by high bare hills |
| •SUGGESTED MAP• | aqua3 OS Explorer OL41 Forest of Bowland & Ribblesdale |
| •START / FINISH• | Grid reference: SD 658468 |
| •DOG FRIENDLINESS• | Grazing land, keep dogs on leads |
| •PARKING• | Roadside parking near Inn at Whitewell or below church |
| •PUBLIC TOILETS• | At Dunsop Bridge (➤ Walk 37) |

## BACKGROUND TO THE WALK

With two sets of stepping stones to cross, this walk could be problematic when the river is in flood – but the good thing is that you will know immediately if this is so. Should this be the case you'll then have the choice of moving elsewhere or simply drowning your sorrows at the Inn at Whitewell.

### Limestone Quarries

Having crossed the river, you climb around the flanks of New Laund Hill and then cross another small ridge into the valley of Dinkling Green Brook. There are several exposures of limestone, mostly the result of quarrying, on the ridge just north of the track. Limestone, which underlies most of the ground covered by the walk, tends to produce good grazing conditions, unlike the more acid soils formed on the gritstone of the higher fells.

As the 'Forest' element in 'Forest of Bowland' suggests, the area was once dominated by hunting, especially of deer. (The name 'laund', as in New Laund, means a hunting park.) 'Forest' does not automatically imply tree-cover, as it does to us today, but the valleys and lower slopes certainly were much more wooded. By the later Middle Ages, however, there was a shift towards farming and trees were cleared to be replaced by pasture for both sheep and cattle.

### An Ancient Ford

Knot Hill Quarry is the largest exposure of limestone on the walk, and marks the start of the descent back towards the second crossing of the Hodder. This is another grand line of stepping stones alongside an ancient ford. Stepping stones are fine for us, after all, but they are of little use to livestock. In medieval times bridging a river like the Hodder was a major undertaking and fords were therefore of great significance. It's no surprise, then, to find another substantial farm immediately beyond the crossing. Stakes is a particularly fine 17th-century farmhouse.

After Stakes the route rises away from the river, but dips back towards it before climbing in earnest. Above a plantation you cross a large open field which has been created from several smaller ones: the faint ridges and furrows of the old field boundaries can still be seen and initially the path follows one of them. Beyond this there's a little more climbing before a green path contours above the valley, giving a great view of the ground you've covered and then, as it swings around, over Whitewell towards Dunsop Bridge and the wilder country beyond.

The final descent takes you past the graveyard. Its separation from the church may strike you as odd – though in many parts of the world this is normal practice. Here it probably results from the limited space around the church and the potential danger of flooding on the level ground below it.

Walk 36

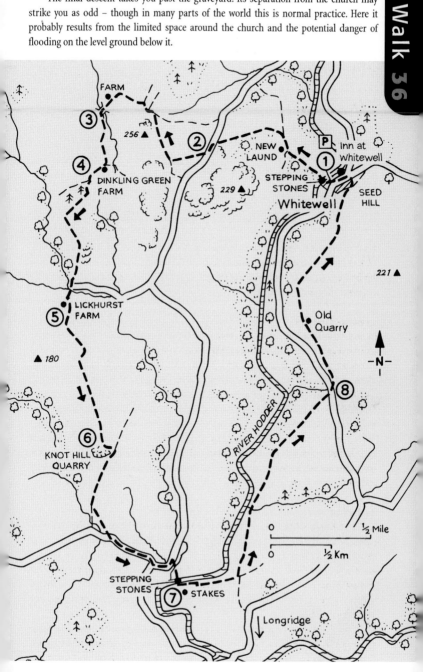

**Walk 36**

## Walk 36 Directions

① From the lower parking area follow the riverbank left to the stepping stones. Climb just right of the woods and straight through the farmyard of **New Laund**. By an old cheese press go left on a curving track below slopes, then up a field. Bear left to a gate into a lane. Go a few paces left to a stile on the right.

---

**WHERE TO EAT AND DRINK** ⓘ

Look no further than the **Inn at Whitewell**. It's enormously popular but there's plenty of room. The main bar is usually very busy yet relaxed, there's good beer on hand pump and the bar food is good, though not cheap.

---

② Cross rough pasture, aiming just left of the house, then go right on the surfaced track, swinging round into another little valley. Go left to a farm, then right, through the farmyard and down to a footbridge.

③ Turn left, past chicken coops, to a stile on the right. Cross a field corner to another stile then straight on to **Dinkling Green Farm**. A gap to the right of the large cow shed leads into the farmyard.

④ Halfway down the yard go right, between buildings, to a ford. Keep left past a plantation, follow the next field edge then go through a gate in a dip. Follow the hedge

---

**WHILE YOU'RE THERE** ⓘ

The **Bowland Wild Boar Park** actually lies within the loop of the walk and its main attraction is exactly what the name suggests. It also has deer, llamas and a variety of smaller animals. **Browsholme Hall** has been in the same family for 600 years, though the building 'only' dates back to 1507.

---

round then cross it and go over a rise. Bear right, down to the beck, then up the lane to **Lickhurst Farm**.

⑤ Turn left into the farmyard then bear right and straight on down a track. When it swings right, go left before the next gate then straight ahead on an intermittent track.

⑥ Just before **Knot Hill Quarry**, turn left, past a limekiln, to a junction. Go right and down to a lane. Go left then left again, round a bend and down. Cross a bridge on the right and head towards **Stakes farm**, crossing the river on more stepping stones.

---

**WHAT TO LOOK FOR** ⓘ

Just below Knot Hill Quarry there's a good example of a **limekiln**. By heating the crushed stone carbon dioxide was driven off leaving fairly pure calcium (lime). This was used for fertiliser, mortar and whitewash. There are fossil-rich blocks in some of the walls, notably on the high path before the final descent.

---

⑦ Turn left and climb above the river. At the next junction go left, descend steeply, then swing right, slightly above the **River Hodder**, to a stile. Follow the fence to another stile, then bear left to a ford. Go up a rough track and keep climbing past the right edge of a plantation. Keep straight on across an open field to a stile in the furthest corner.

⑧ Across the road, a few paces left, is a gate. Bear left to iron gates. Contour round the hill, just above the fence, to more gates. After 100yds (91m) go down through an aluminium gate. The track swings right. Just past **Seed Hill** turn left and descend steps by the graveyard. A short steep lane descends back to the start.

# Moors at the Centre

*A tough walk that gives a chance to taste the freedom of the high moors.*

| | |
|---|---|
| •DISTANCE• | 9¼ miles (14.9km) |
| •MINIMUM TIME• | 3hrs 30min |
| •ASCENT / GRADIENT• | 1,247ft (380m) ▲▲▲ |
| •LEVEL OF DIFFICULTY• | 🕅🕅 🕅🕅 🕅🕅 |
| •PATHS• | Field paths, rougher moorland paths, surfaced road, 9 stiles |
| •LANDSCAPE• | Rough pasture, exposed moorland, sheltered valley |
| •SUGGESTED MAP• | aqua3 OS Explorer OL41 Forest of Bowland & Ribblesdale |
| •START / FINISH• | Grid reference: SD 660501 |
| •DOG FRIENDLINESS• | Grazing land, keep dogs on leads |
| •PARKING• | Public car park at Dunsop Bridge |
| •PUBLIC TOILETS• | At car park |

## BACKGROUND TO THE WALK

There aren't many places where a phone box is a tourist attraction, but the one at Dunsop Bridge is deemed to stand at the centre point of Great Britain. This apart, Dunsop Bridge lacks amusements for less energetic visitors, but it lacks nothing for magnificent surroundings and is the starting point for many great walks. This route uses something which is quite a rarity in Bowland, a public footpath crossing the tops.

### To the Tops
To reach it you cross a stretch of upland pasture. This gives straightforward walking, rarely steep, except where it dips into Oxenhurst Clough. The clough frames a view of the small conical hill called Knot or Sugar Loaf, which began as a coral reef around 250 million years ago. The ascent to the plateau is by a well-defined ridge, giving wider views than from the level top. The prospect takes in the Hodder Valley, Stocks Reservoir and Gisburn Forest, the broader sweep of Ribblesdale and the Yorkshire hills.

### Heather Moors
The heather moors of Bowland have traditionally been managed principally for grouse shooting. In recent years, for reasons that are not fully understood, grouse numbers have declined substantially. This has affected the livelihood of many local people and has had a knock-on effect on other species. Hen harriers, for instance, prey in part on grouse chicks.

### The Birds of Bowland Project
In the past walkers, conservationists and shooting interests have sometimes viewed each other suspiciously. Gamekeepers have been accused of poisoning birds of prey. Today, however, there is a new spirit of co-operation. The Birds of Bowland Project involves the RSPB, United Utilities (a major landowner) and receives funding from the Heritage Lottery Fund and Ribble Valley District Council. The aim is to encourage sympathetic management of the distinctive habitat and to protect the bird populations. One result should be to encourage more visitors to the area, something which should be further helped by the much wider access to open country which is due to be achieved by 2005.

The moorland crossing may seem all too brief before the descent into Whitendale. Here there are reminders that Bowland is a significant water catchment. Although there's only one large reservoir (Stocks), water is extracted from many of the streams and rivers. The track which you join near Whitendale Farm is actually the line of a water pipe: BCWW stands for Blackburn Corporation Water Works. The main waterworks intake is a little further down the valley and from there you follow the access road most of the way back to Dunsop Bridge.

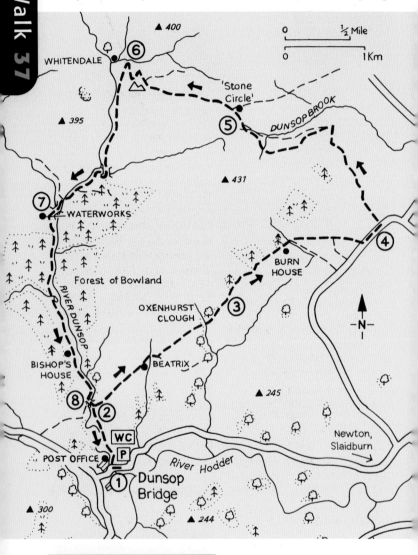

## Walk 37 Directions

① From the public car park in Dunsop Bridge, go up a surfaced track, just to the left of the **post office** and tea room, for about 800yds (732m). When you reach the end of the track, by some houses, follow a public footpath for another 100yds (91m) then go right, up a steep bank.

② Cross the large field, bearing slightly left to meet power lines. Continue to a stile just before **Beatrix farm**. Follow the track round the farm until it swings back right again. Go left, through the second of two gates. Climb the slope right of a small stream, over a stile, then follow a wire fence across the hillside. Drop into **Oxenhurst Clough** then climb out through a plantation, rejoining the fence as the gradient eases. Keep straight on to join another track.

③ Follow the track for ¾ mile (1.2km) to **Burn House**, where it swings right. Bear away left, across an open field, towards the middle of a young plantation. Follow the path through it, bearing right to a stile. Aim just right of another young plantation in a dip, then across a field towards some houses (**Laythams**). Go left on the lane for 300yds (274m).

④ Turn left up a metalled track. Clearly marked gates guide you round a house. About 50yds (46m) above this, drop to the stream and continue up to its left. From the top of the enclosure a path rises to the right alongside an obvious groove, then swings back left. Climb steadily up a ridge and then swing rightwards above the upper reaches of **Dunsop Brook**. Cross a broad plateau, roughly parallel to an old wall, to a circular patch of stones.

⑤ Turn left and cross the wall at a stile. The path ahead is rough but always clear. After a slight rise it starts to descend, gently at first but gradually getting steeper. As the ground really steepens, descend in big zig-zags, with a gate halfway down. Just above the farm at **Whitendale** go left.

⑥ Follow a conspicuously level track for ¾ mile (1.2km) until it swings round a little side valley, over a couple of footbridges. Go over a stile and wind down to a track by the river. Follow this down to a bridge by some **waterworks**.

⑦ Cross the bridge, join the road and follow it steadily down the valley for 1½ miles (2.4km), past **Bishop's House**.

⑧ Just after a cattle grid, cross the river on a substantial footbridge. Just beyond this you rejoin the outward route.

# Maybe Middle-Earth: Hurst Green and Three Rivers

**Walk 38**

*Did these rivers, fields and woods inspire Tolkien's creation of The Shire?*

| | |
|---|---|
| •DISTANCE• | 6½ miles (10.4km) |
| •MINIMUM TIME• | 2hrs |
| •ASCENT / GRADIENT• | 459ft (14m) ▲▲ ▲ ▲ |
| •LEVEL OF DIFFICULTY• | 🚶🚶 🚶🚶 🚶 |
| •PATHS• | Grassy riverside paths, woodland and farm tracks, 11 stiles |
| •LANDSCAPE• | Pastoral scenery, scattered woodlands, backdrop of moors |
| •SUGGESTED MAP• | aqua3 OS Explorer 287 West Pennine Moors |
| •START / FINISH• | Grid reference: SD 684382 |
| •DOG FRIENDLINESS• | Can run free in woodland sections |
| •PARKING• | By Hurst Green village hall or on roadside adjacent |
| •PUBLIC TOILETS• | Centre of Hurst Green |

## BACKGROUND TO THE WALK

You don't have to be a Tolkien fan to enjoy this walk, which has long been recognised as a logical and graceful outing.

### Tolkien Connection

Recent research by Jonathan Hewat (a teacher at Stonyhurst's prep school, St Mary's Hall) has uncovered the extent of the Tolkien connection. This much is certain: J R R Tolkien, author of *The Lord of the Rings*, knew this area well. One of his sons studied for the priesthood at Stonyhurst and Tolkien spent long periods here while he was writing the trilogy. The rest, though fascinating, is largely conjecture. In the hobbits' Shire there's a River Shirebourn, and the Shireburn family once owned Stonyhurst. But does that mean that Hurst Green is Hobbiton?

### Ribble Valley

Tolkien also drew great inspiration from the country of his boyhood in the West Midlands, deeply regretting its disappearance under roads and factories. Perhaps the enduringly green Ribble Valley reminded him of that lost landscape. No doubt The Shire owes something to both. If the Tolkien angle intrigues you, a locally available leaflet gives much more detail.

Just after reaching the Ribble, you pass the graceful aqueduct, built in 1880 to supply water to Blackburn. An easy ³/₄ mile (1.2km) brings you to Jumbles Rocks, outcrops of limestone which form natural weirs and a ford. The ford has been used, when the water's low, since time immemorial. Until the 1950s there was also a ferry and the isolated Boat House was the ferryman's home.

In the fields near by are two obvious mounds. The lower one was excavated in 1894 and dated to around 1250 BC. The larger, though known to be artificial, has yet to be properly examined. As the Ribble swings round, the River Calder enters opposite, close to 17th-century Hacking Hall. Less than ³/₄ mile (1.2km) further on is the confluence of the Ribble and the Hodder, which you follow briefly before leaving it near Winckley Hall.

You'll soon return to the river at Low Hodder Bridge. Just downstream is the ancient Cromwell's Bridge – a misplaced name. The bridge was actually built for one of the Shireburn dynasty in 1562. Legend has it that Cromwell vandalised it, destroying the parapets that impeded the progress of his troops.

### The Northern Lights

You follow the Hodder for almost another mile (1.6km) before climbing steeply away to Woodfields. Tolkien stayed in one of these houses. The track passes St Mary's Hall and then reaches Hall Barn Farm. Near by, on the edge of the college precincts is a small observatory. This was one of a network, observations from which helped the Norwegian physicist Kristian Birkeland confirm the magnetic origin of the Northern Lights.

**Walk 38**

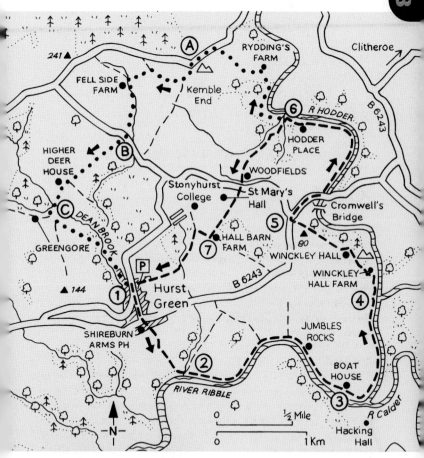

## Walk 38 Directions

① Walk down the road to the centre of Hurst Green village. Cross the main road and go down left of the **Shireburn Arms** to a stile below the main car park. Go down the edge of a field then follow a small stream to some duckboards and a footbridge. After a slight rise, wooden steps wind down to the **River Ribble**. Bear left just above the river.

Walk 38

② Skirt the aqueduct and return to the river bank. A gravel track swings right past **Jumbles Rocks**. Go through a gate alongside a small stone building with a mast to rejoin the river bank and follow it, towards the **Boat House**.

③ After rounding the big bend, go up slightly to a track. Follow this for about ½ mile (800m). Opposite the confluence of the Ribble and the Hodder, go over a stile by a bench.

> **WHERE TO EAT AND DRINK** ⓘ
> In the absence of a Green Dragon or Prancing Pony, the **Shireburn Arms** has the most Tolkeinesque name, and it's a very comfortable place, if a little bit upmarket for hobbits. (You'll probably want to change out of muddy boots first.) There's a smart restaurant as well as a good range of bar food.

④ The narrow path quickly rejoins the track. At **Winckley Hall Farm** go left to the houses, right between barns then left past a pond and out into a lane. This climbs steeply then levels out, swinging left past **Winckley Hall**. Go through a kissing gate on the right and across the field to another. Keep straight on across a large field, just left of a wood, then down past a pond and up to a road.

⑤ Turn right down a pavement to the river. Immediately before the bridge, turn left along a track.

> **WHILE YOU'RE THERE** ⓘ
> **Stonyhurst College** was originally the home of the Shireburn family and much of the original Elizabethan house still exists, though almost enveloped by vast 19th-century additions. It was taken over in 1794 by Jesuits fleeing the French Revolution and is now a leading Catholic boarding school. It's open to visitors during the summer holidays.

Follow the river round, climb up past **Hodder Place** then descend again to a bridge over a stream.

⑥ Go up the track on the left, cross a footbridge then climb a long flight of wooden steps. Follow the top edge of a plantation then cross a stile into a field. Keep to its edge and at the end cross a stile into a stony track. Keep left, past **Woodfields** and out to the road. Go down the track by the post-box to **Hall Barn Farm** and along the right side of the buildings.

⑦ Turn right on a tarmac track for 200yds (183m). Go left through a gate by the end of a wall and along a narrow field. At its end go right to a track alongside a wood then up to a kissing gate. Follow the field edge to another kissing gate. At the top of the final field, through a gate, a narrow path leads to a short lane. At its end turn left back to the start.

> **WHAT TO LOOK FOR** ⓘ
> One plant to look out for, especially along the riversides, is **butterbur**. This is another name that will ring bells with Tolkien devotees; there's an innkeeper in *The Lord of the Rings* called Barliman Butterbur. The flower spikes, which appear in early spring, look superficially like dull pinkish hyacinths, but the individual flowers are daisy-like. Later in the year huge leaves develop, these were traditionally used to wrap butter.

# Over Birdy Brow

*An extension taking in woodlands, a fine viewpoint and a secret dell.*
**See map and information panel for Walk 38**

| | |
|---|---|
| •DISTANCE• | 8 miles (12.9km) |
| •MINIMUM TIME• | 2hrs 45min |
| •ASCENT / GRADIENT• | 804ft (245m) ▲▲▲ |
| •LEVEL OF DIFFICULTY• | 🚶 🚶 🚶 |
| •SUGGESTED MAP• | aqua3 OS Explorers 287 West Pennine Moors; OL41 Forest of Bowland & Ribblesdale |

## Walk 39 Directions
## (Walk 38 option)

From the small bridge at Point ⑥, climb the wooden steps parallel to the river then take the footpath on the right to a stone cross. Beyond this the lower path turns out easier, after the initial scramble down over tree roots. The paths rejoin as the slope eases.

On emerging from the wood turn left, and head straight up the hill to a stile on the skyline left of the prominent house (**Rydding's Farm**). Go left on the track for 400yds (366m) then go left across the field to a power line pole. Go up left to a gate and out into the road (known as **Birdy Brow**). Climb it steeply then, just below the zig-zag (Point Ⓐ), go left along a track.

Follow the track round past the first house and then back left. Cross two stiles left of **Lowfield Cottage**. From the corner of the farm, bear right up the hill just right of trees that appear, to a stile. Slant right across the field corner. Over the fence in the next field is the ancient Paulinus or **Kemple End Cross**.

Follow the fence, then a wall, to the left. From the next stile descend towards the right side of **Fell Side Farm**. Go over two stiles then straight down, left of **Fell Side Barn**. Keep straight on, joining a track in a dip alongside a stream. Follow the track to the road by a cottage (Point Ⓑ).

Go right 70yds (64m) then go left on the track to **Higher Deer House**. Go through a gate at the end, slightly left to another, then across the field to a stile above the wooded valley of **Dean Brook**. Descend to a footbridge (Point Ⓒ) then bear left, zig-zagging back right halfway up. At the top keep right to a stile in the corner then follow a narrow path to a track. Just above is **Greengore**, used as a hunting lodge in the 16th and 17th centuries.

Go left 150yds (137m) then left again on a narrower path. Follow this down to a bridge and continue down the main track above the **Dean Brook**. Where the track forks take the lower one. Just past the first cottages there's a stile on the right. Follow the narrow path to another tarmac lane and go left, emerging almost opposite the **Bayley Arms**. Turn right back to the **village hall**.

# Clitheroe's River and Castle

*Partly a town trail, but mostly a rural walk beside the River Ribble.*

| | |
|---|---|
| •DISTANCE• | 3½ miles (5.7km) |
| •MINIMUM TIME• | 1hr 15min |
| •ASCENT / GRADIENT• | 164ft (50m) ▲ ▲ ▲ |
| •LEVEL OF DIFFICULTY• | 🏃 🏃 🏃 |
| •PATHS• | Field paths, surfaced tracks, pavement, 7 stiles |
| •LANDSCAPE• | Urban, rural, woodland and riverside – a rare mix! |
| •SUGGESTED MAP• | aqua3 OS Explorer OL41 Forest of Bowland & Ribblesdale |
| •START / FINISH• | Grid reference: SD 744422 |
| •DOG FRIENDLINESS• | Can roam free in Brungerley Park, on leads elsewhere |
| •PARKING• | Long stay car park on Chester Avenue, by Clitheroe Station |
| •PUBLIC TOILETS• | On Church Walk |

## Walk 40 Directions

Walk towards the railway then bear right on a road blocked to through traffic. Follow it round to **Kirkmoor Road** and go right. At **Back Commons** go over a stile. Cross the field to another stile, bear right to a kissing gate and immediately right through another. From a third gate go right on a short track past the cemetery to the road and go left for 250yds (229m).

Go right, up the lane then, just past the gates of **Park Hill**, go left on a footpath. Cross the field to the edge of the wood. Go down left then swing right on a surfaced track. Follow this for about 150yds (137m) then descend to river level near to the boundary of the **Cross Hill Nature Reserve**.

The reserve centres on **Cross Hill Quarry**, which ceased working in the 1900s. Like others in the area it once served the cement industry (which is still active, as you'll see). The woods near the river produce

masses of wood anemones by early March: these star-like white flowers are among the earliest signs of spring. From below the quarry follow the riverbank for about ¾ mile (1.2km) to **Bradford Bridge**, near the huge cement works, the one large-scale industrial plant in the pastoral Ribble Valley.

Cross the bridge and, from the bend in the road, follow the river bank through the first field, then go diagonally right to a stile. Keep left where other paths branch off, then cross a larger field to a concrete footbridge. Bear left across the next field, quite near the river again, then join a farm track up a rise and bear right past **Brungerley Farm** to the road.

### WHILE YOU'RE THERE ⓘ

The **Castle Museum** seems larger on the inside than it does on the outside, and is good on geology as well as history. Don't miss the **Geological Trail** at Salthill Quarry on the outskirts of the town. Clitheroe has good **shopping** too – lovers of sausages and/or wine will be in seventh heaven.

> **WHAT TO LOOK FOR** ℹ
>
> Clitheroe is built on **limestone**, which is visible at Cross Hill Quarry, in the riverbed and in the knoll on which the Castle stands. Many of the town's buildings are of limestone too, but darker gritstone also appears, quarried a short distance away (there are still active quarries on Waddington Fell, for instance). When you walk down Kirkmoor Road, the terraced houses on one side are built of gritstone while those opposite are built of limestone.

Go left across **Brungerley Bridge**. Go over the wall by the bus shelter and down the steps. Follow the river bank to a gate into **Boy Bank Wood**. Ignore an obvious line of steps on the left and follow a level, though rougher, path to the large weir opposite **Waddow Hall**. On the far side is a fish ladder, and on our side an old sluice gate. The canal, now partly silted up, ran for about ½ mile (800m) to the large mill at **Low Moor**, formerly owned by the Garnett family of Waddow Hall.

Beyond the sluice the steep bank on the left begins to diminish. Go up and back left along the top of the bank, to meet a clear path (coming up from the steps you passed a few minutes ago). Turn sharp right across the field to the end of a line of trees and a kissing gate. Follow the left edge of the next field. At the next gate you briefly rejoin the outward route, going slightly right to a stile and across the last field to **Back Commons**.

Keep straight on down **Kirkmoor Road**, swing right and out to a busier road. Cross the railway bridge. From the end of its parapet double back to the right, under the little footbridge that serves the Methodist chapel.

Enter the castle grounds and turn left immediately up a rising road. Near its crest go left up a stepped path. At its top go up steps on the left then turn right immediately below the buildings. At their end go up more steps, emerging in front of the **Castle Museum**.

From the museum entrance go up again, then bear right through the yard, towards the keep. Go up steps, then left into the keep. Leave by the other 'door'. Immediately to its right are more steps giving access to the ramparts and a great view.

> **WHERE TO EAT AND DRINK** ℹ
>
> The **Swan and Royal**, on Castle Street has well-kept Jennings ales and a good range of bar food – try the baguettes – as well as a children's menu. If alcohol isn't essential, the **Exchange Coffee Company**, on Wellgate, also does excellent lunches and delicious cakes.

From the base of these steps go right down a stepped path. Keep right at the bottom, out into **Castle Street**. The distinctive wedge-shaped building at the end of the street is now the town library, but in its time it has also been town hall, police station, lock-up, and public lavatories! The area in front of it was the original market-place, but it's a very cramped site. Markets used to overflow into Castle Street and Church Street; maybe they would again if only Castle Street were closed to traffic.

An arch beside the **White Lion** leads into **Church Walk**. Go left at the bottom, then right, to the railway station. The main building is now a gallery, but the railway is still busy, with trains to Manchester. Go right 50yds (46m) and under the tracks to return to the car park.

**Walk 41**

# Breezy Brine Fields of Knott End

*An easy walk exploring an unexpected and curiously salty corner of Lancashire's coastal plain.*

| | |
|---|---|
| •DISTANCE• | 5½ miles (8.8km) |
| •MINIMUM TIME• | 1hr 45min |
| •ASCENT / GRADIENT• | 115ft (35m) ▲ ▲ ▲ |
| •LEVEL OF DIFFICULTY• | 🚶 🚶 🚶 |
| •PATHS• | Quiet streets and lanes, farm tracks and sea wall, 3 stiles |
| •LANDSCAPE• | Short built-up section, seashore, farmland and golf course |
| •SUGGESTED MAP• | aqua3 OS Explorer 296 Lancaster, Morecambe & Fleetwood |
| •START / FINISH• | Grid reference: SD 347485 |
| •DOG FRIENDLINESS• | Can run free on sea wall, under close control elsewhere |
| •PARKING• | Free car park by end of B5270 at Knott End |
| •PUBLIC TOILETS• | At side of coastguard building adjacent to car park |

## BACKGROUND TO THE WALK

The salt industry in this part of Lancashire is not of the same antiquity as that in Cheshire and has not had the same profound impact on the landscape, but it still played a significant part in shaping the present scene.

### Rock Salt

Extensive deposits of rock salt lie below the surface around Knott End and Preesall. In the early days of the industry, natural brine was found but more commonly it is extracted by pumping fresh water down bore holes to dissolve the rock salt. The first such wells in this area were drilled in the 1890s and many of the well-heads can still be seen, often standing incongruously in the middle of green fields surrounded by contentedly grazing Friesians.

### Chemical Foundations

The brine fields provided the raw material on which the ICI Hillhouse chemical plant, just across the Wyre, was founded, producing chlorine as well as salt. This has developed subsequently to produce a much wider range of chemical products.

There's no feel of an industrial town about Knott End today, which is a mixture of modest resort and commuter village. At low tide the sands are exposed for miles, far out into Morecambe Bay, and when it's clear the Lakeland skyline makes a wonderful backdrop.

### Pilling Pig

As you leave the built-up area, you meet the trackbed of the railway line that once linked Knott End to the main line at Garstang. The line was affectionately known as 'The Pilling Pig', a name derived from the note of the whistle of an early engine. The section to Pilling was opened in 1870 but the extension to Knott End had to wait until 1908. It closed in 1963.

When you leave the old trackbed you climb a small rise – almost the only one you'll encounter on the whole walk – and from the far side, beyond New Heys Farm, you get your

**Walk 41**

first sighting of the brine fields. To begin with they may look like nothing more than ordinary farmland, but then you will notice several pools – the walk soon passes close by one – left by subsidence.

### Creeks and Salt Marsh

As the walk continues, you'll see more and more reminders of the salt industry, especially along the track from the lane out to the sea wall. You follow this northward, with extensive creeks and salt marsh off to the left, and views across the Wyre to the chemical works and to Fleetwood.

Flying golf balls add spice to the next part of the walk. There's an interlude as you pass Hackensall Hall. The present building was erected in 1656 by the Fleetwood family, but later passed into the hands of the Bournes and was extensively renovated in the 19th century. There's more golf course to cross before returning to the sea wall for the last short stretch.

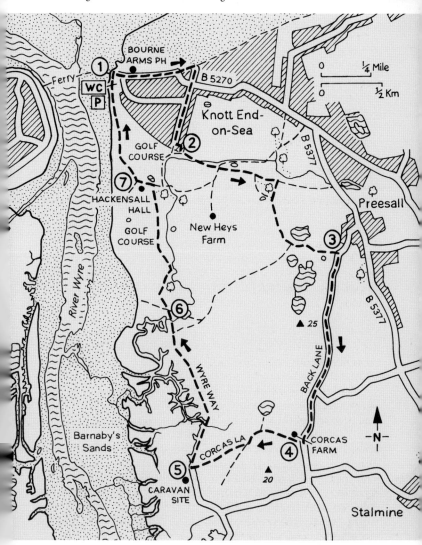

Walk 41

# Walk 41 Directions

① Go out to the sea wall, turn right past the ferry, along the road past the **Bourne Arms** and then along the **Esplanade**. Where the main road swings away, keep on along the seafront, down a private road then a short stretch of footpath. Where this ends, before a grassy stretch of seafront, go right down a short side-street then straight across the main road into **Hackensall Road**. Go down this almost to its end.

② Just before the last house on the left there's a footpath (sign high up on lamppost) which wriggles round and then becomes a clear straight track. Follow this through a narrow belt of woodland, across open fields and then alongside a wooded slope. Where the wood ends go through an iron kissing gate on the right then up the edge of the wood and over a stile into a farmyard. Go straight through this and down a stony track, which swings left between pools. It then becomes a surfaced lane past some cottages.

### WHERE TO EAT AND DRINK

There's a **café** adjacent to the car park and a couple of others in the village. The **Bourne Arms** is close by; a large pub with a conservatory at the back, and generous portions of pub food to enjoy.

③ Join a wider road (**Back Lane**) and go right. It becomes narrow again. Follow this lane for about a mile (1.6km), over a slight rise and down again, to **Corcas Farm**.

④ Turn right on **Corcas Lane**, signed 'Private Road Bridle Path Only'. Follow the lane through the brine fields. After ½ mile (800m) it swings left by a caravan site.

⑤ Go right, past a Wyre Way sign and over a stile on to the embankment. Follow its winding course for about a mile (1.6km) to a stile with a signpost just beyond.

### WHILE YOU'RE THERE

For most of the year, a small passenger ferry regularly makes the short crossing to **Fleetwood**. The town was planned as an integrated whole in the 1830s and 40s by the architect Decimus Burton, at the instigation of Sir Peter Hesketh-Fleetwood from nearby Rossall Estate. The Fleetwood Museum tells much more about the salt industry. Britain's oldest surviving tram system links Fleetwood with Blackpool.

⑥ Go straight ahead on a tractor track, signed 'Public Footpath to Hackensall Hall 1m'. When it meets the **golf course**, the track first follows its left side then angles across – heed the danger signs! Follow the track to the right of **Hackensall Hall**. Just past its main gates go left on a track with a Wyre Way sign. This skirts round behind the outlying buildings.

⑦ The path swings to the right and then crosses the **golf course** again. Aim for a green shelter on the skyline then bear right along the edge of the course. Skirt round some white cottages, then go left to the sea wall. Turn right along it, and it's just a drive and a chip back to the car park.

### WHAT TO LOOK FOR

The well-heads, pools, and one small extraction plant all bear witness to the salt industry. The fields provide good grazing for dairy cattle and also for a large number of **brown hares**. They are larger than rabbits, with longer legs and ears. They don't burrow but rear their young in shallow scrapes in the ground.

# The Bottom and the Top: Around Beacon Fell

*A very popular slice of upland Lancashire countryside, by turns both expansive and intimate.*

| | |
|---|---|
| •DISTANCE• | 6 miles (9.7km) |
| •MINIMUM TIME• | 2hrs |
| •ASCENT / GRADIENT• | 689ft (210m)   ▲▲▲ |
| •LEVEL OF DIFFICULTY• | 👫 👫 👫 |
| •PATHS• | Field paths, in places indistinct, clear tracks, 19 stiles |
| •LANDSCAPE• | Forest, heathland, farmland, woodland, riverside |
| •SUGGESTED MAP• | aqua3 OS Explorer OL41 Forest of Bowland & Ribblesdale |
| •START / FINISH• | Grid reference: SD 565426 |
| •DOG FRIENDLINESS• | Dogs may run free on Beacon Fell and in Brock Valley |
| •PARKING• | By Beacon Fell visitor centre |
| •PUBLIC TOILETS• | At visitor centre |

## BACKGROUND TO THE WALK

With a name like Beacon Fell, you'd expect a prominent hill, and it is. An outlier of the Bowland Fells, its altitude of 873ft (266m) may seem comparatively modest but its detached position gives excellent sight lines – and it was much more accessible for those who had to man the beacon!

### Part of a Network

In the days before telegraph and telephone, beacons were the nearest thing to instantaneous communication. Admittedly they couldn't convey any detail, but they did serve to warn of great events. Most famously, a network of hundreds of beacons – of which this was one – spread the news of the appearance of the Spanish Armada in 1588.

From this history, and some contemporary publicity, you might reasonably expect 360 degree views, but at the present time stands of conifers block out the southern half of the panorama. However, you get much of the 'missing' half anyway, early in the walk, as you descend the southern flank of the hill. Preston figures prominently. Alongside the anonymous tower blocks are the Preston North End football stadium at Deepdale and the slender spire of St Walburge's Roman Catholic Church, the tallest church spire in Britain after Salisbury Cathedral.

### Brock Bottom

You wend your way across farmland, pleasantly enough, and then drop abruptly into the enclosed valley of the River Brock, usually referred to as Brock Bottom. A paper mill existed here in 1786, but was replaced soon after by a larger cotton mill. The mill site is just downstream when you reach the river, while on the way upstream you'll see remains of the millstream, dam and sluices. Since the mill closed in 1923, the valley has been popular with Preston folk. In the days when a bicycle was the most likely means of transport it was a handy distance from the town.

From the bridge at Brock Mill (don't be confused; this is not the main mill site previously referred to) you climb again. Rougher pastures, ill-drained and with large stands of rushes, intervene before the steeper climb through forest on to the upper slopes of Beacon Fell. Here there are large open areas, now being managed as heathland.

The summit view may expand with forest clearance in years to come but even now the half that you can see is grand. Mostly it's a fairly local prospect, over Bleasedale to the higher Bowland Fells. These rise to 1,673ft (510m) at Fair Snape Fell, but the most prominent is the abrupt end of Parlick. When the wind is right you'll usually see hang-gliders here and there's a gliding club based just below.

There's also an enticing slice of the Lakeland skyline, stretching from the dark whaleback of Black Combe to Dow Crag and Coniston Old Man, behind which Scafell and England's highest, Scafell Pike, appear.

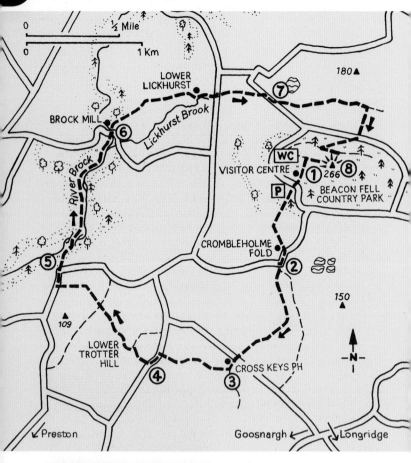

## Walk 42 **Directions**

① Look for a public footpath sign in the left-hand corner of the car park by the **visitor centre**. Go down the broad track, then through a field. Bear left towards **Crombleholme Fold** and walk through the farmyard, emerging on to a minor country lane. Turn right to reach a bend.

### WHERE TO EAT AND DRINK ⓘ

It's a couple of miles (3.2km) in the direction of Goosnargh to the **Horns Inn**, an attractive old place that does good honest pub food. There's a non-smoking dining room. Beer-lovers might want to continue that bit further into Goosnargh village and the **Grapes**, which also serves food all day.

② Go left, cross a stream then up a track swinging right. After 50yds (46m) go left, slanting gently down to a stile just before the field ends. From another stile, 15yds (14m) further on, go down a field then angle right to a low bridge and straight up the track beyond.

③ Go through the **Cross Keys** car park, through a farmyard and into a field. Go right to a stile then straight on to the corner of a hedge. Follow it to a tree then angle left to a stile. Go right then straight ahead to a lane and go left.

### WHILE YOU'RE THERE ⓘ

**Longridge** is a modest town with a few specialist shops. A little further away, on the banks of the River Ribble, is **Ribchester**. This is one of the most important Roman sites in Lancashire, with a nicely-presented museum. The White Bull Inn, at the stone-built heart of the village, has pillars which probably originated in a Roman bathhouse.

④ Go right to **Lower Trotter Hill**. Cross a cattle grid, go left, then round to the right and past a house. Go through the left-hand gate and up to a stile. Follow the field edge, eventually bending left. Go down a stony track and right on a road.

⑤ As the road bends to the right keep walking straight ahead. Descend a sunken track through woods and cross a footbridge. Go up a few paces, then right, and follow obvious paths near the river to **Brock Mill**.

⑥ Cross the bridge then go through a gateway on the left. Bear right up a track then go right, through rhododendrons. Follow the edge of a wood, then go right, crossing the stream. Go up a field edge and straight on towards **Lower Lickhurst**. Go round into the drive and up to the road. Go left for just a few paces, then go right, up a drive. Keep straight on as it bends left, up fields to a lane. Go right for 140yds (128m).

⑦ Go left over a stile and diagonally to an isolated thorn tree. Continue almost level to a gateway and then to a stile and footbridge. Follow an old boundary, now a muddy depression, then bear left to power lines. Follow these to a marker post. Go right, directly uphill. Cross the road to a track rising through forest. At a junction go left for 200m (183m) then right up a narrow path to the summit trig point.

⑧ Bear right along the edge of the forest then left across a boardwalk. Keep straight on to return directly to the **visitor centre**.

### WHAT TO LOOK FOR ⓘ

There are three main classes of 'grass-like' plant. True **grasses** have round, hollow stems (bamboo is a grass). **Sedges** have solid stems with a triangular section. They are mostly found in damp or infertile soils – many of the 'grasses' on the moors are actually sedges. Finally, **rushes** have round solid stems. The soft rush is a common example. It grows in damp places but its clumps usually provide a sound footing.

Walk 43

# Picturesque Crook O'Lune

*A well-loved local beauty spot, but beauty isn't just skin-deep.*

| | |
|---|---|
| •DISTANCE• | 3¼ miles (5.3km) |
| •MINIMUM TIME• | 1hr |
| •ASCENT / GRADIENT• | 164ft (50m) ▲▲▲ |
| •LEVEL OF DIFFICULTY• | 👣👣 👣👣 👣👣 |
| •PATHS• | Tracks, pavement, woodland and field paths, 5 stiles |
| •LANDSCAPE• | Great river bend, steep woods and open valley |
| •SUGGESTED MAP• | aqua3 OS Explorer OL41 Forest of Bowland & Ribblesdale |
| •START / FINISH• | Grid reference: SD 521647 |
| •DOG FRIENDLINESS• | Care needed on cycleway and road, can run free elsewhere |
| •PARKING• | At Crook O'Lune, just off A683 |
| •PUBLIC TOILETS• | At car park |

## BACKGROUND TO THE WALK

L andscapes change, and so do the ways people look at them. Rivers change their courses, for instance, although at Crook O'Lune, the river has followed much the same route since the last ice age. It's what geographers call an incised meander, where the river has cut down into solid rock. Further upstream, the valley floor is composed of clay, sand and gravel and the river can shift course much more easily. You get a great view of the Crook from the first bridge. Looking upstream, the hill peeping over the trees is Clougha Pike (▶ Walk 46).

You leave the river to visit Gray's Seat, named for Thomas Gray. Best known as a poet, Gray was also a leader of the Picturesque movement. In the 18th century fashionable gentlefolk began to travel widely. Some of the first guidebooks instructed them precisely where to observe the best views and how to judge them. As the name 'Picturesque' suggests, the real landscape was judged largely on its fitness to make a picture. Gray visited here in 1769. Here's a sample of his pronouncement:

> *'...in the richest of vallies, the Lune serpentizes for many a mile, and comes forth ample and clear, through a well-wooded and richly-pastured foreground. Every feature which constitutes a perfect landscape of the extensive sort is here not only boldly marked but also in its best position'*

You can at least form an impression of the view Gray saw, but much has changed. Half a century later, the great artist J M W Turner also visited; his painting shows a far less wooded foreground (and no caravan site).

After completing the swing round Crook O'Lune, you break out into the wider valley above. Lush riverside pastures give easy walking, with the distinctive outline of Ingleborough forming 'the background of the prospect,' in Gray's terms. You cross the river on a waterworks bridge, built in 1881, carrying water from the Lake District to Manchester. Looking upstream, you can see that the river 'serpentizes'. The map shows it more clearly. It also shows how rights of way don't always follow the present-day river bank. Older maps show how the river has changed its course. (Walk 44 covers this ground).

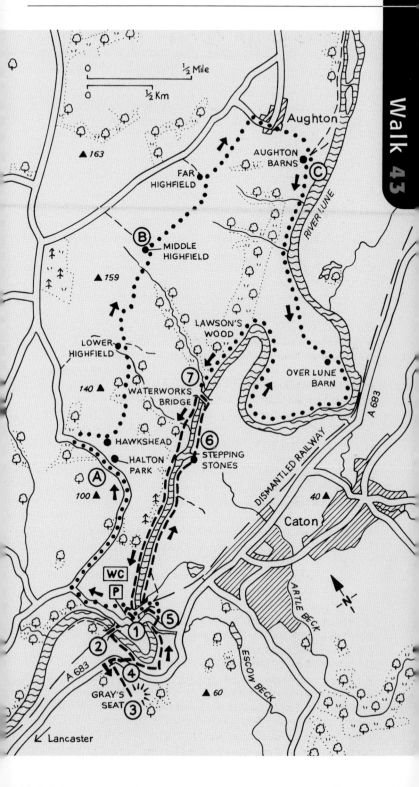

**Walk 43**

## Walk 43 Directions

① From the corner of the car park go down shallow steps to the old railway line. Turn right, under the road, along a short shady track, then cross a bridge high above the river. Go down steps to the right then double back under the bridge you've just crossed.

② Follow a well-trodden path close to the river bank until a steep path with occasional steps leads up to the right. At the top there's a signpost. Go right to a gate, cross the road, and then continue right for 150yds (137m) to a gap in a stone wall on the left. There's a sign for Gray's Seat and an information panel. Follow the enclosed path, with a few rocky steps, to **Gray's Seat**.

> **WHILE YOU'RE THERE** ⓘ
> Just a few miles away is the small town of **Carnforth**. Many of the exterior shots in the classic movie *Brief Encounter* (1945) were filmed at the railway station here. Sadly, it has been neglected for many years but refurbishment has now moved into its final stages.

③ Return down the enclosed path to the road, back along the pavement, and cross again, back to the signpost.

④ Go right, initially level and almost parallel to the road but soon descending, with more steps, back towards the river. The path levels out and then forks. Swing left through a fine grove of beech trees, and over a small footbridge and a stile as you leave the woods. Follow the path along the river bank. A small side stream (**Escow Beck**) can usually be paddled across but if it's too high go round to the right.

Higher up it runs in a culvert. Go up to a kissing gate, cross the road, and go through a gate almost directly opposite.

> **WHERE TO EAT AND DRINK** ⓘ
> **Woody's tea wagon** can be found at the car park every day during the summer and at weekends from November to March, and if you like bacon butties there's no need to look any further.

⑤ Bear left down towards the river, over a footbridge, then round to the right under the old railway bridge. It's easy going now, following the river bank upstream for over ¾ mile (1.2km) to **Artle Beck**. This is crossed by stepping stones.

⑥ Continue up the river bank for 440yds (402m) to the waterworks bridge. Go round to a stile at the far side of the small building, through a kissing gate and up the steps. Cross the catwalk.

⑦ At the end of the bridge drop down left. (A diversion into the first wood is worth the effort, especially in the bluebell season.) Follow the river bank briefly then bear right to a bridge. Keep on the level across the next field to a stile at its far end. Go over this into another wood and follow a clear path through it. All that remains is to follow the river bank back to the bridges and the car park.

> **WHAT TO LOOK FOR** ⓘ
> Birds which can be seen flying low over the water on the first upstream stretch are **sand martins**, related to the swallow. They nest in holes in the sandy banks, almost beneath your feet in some places – so tread lightly. This is a great **salmon** river: you may see anglers and you may see salmon and once in a while you may even see one catch the other.

# High Fields and River Banks

*A longer walk which climbs above the valley for a much wider view.*
**See map and information panel for Walk 43**

| | | |
|---|---|---|
| **•DISTANCE•** | 8¼ miles (13.3km) | |
| **•MINIMUM TIME•** | 3hrs | |
| **•ASCENT / GRADIENT•** | 590ft (100m) | ▲▲▲ |
| **•LEVEL OF DIFFICULTY•** | 🚶🚶 🚶🚶 🚶 | |

## Walk 44 Directions
## (Walk 43 option)

After crossing the road at Point ⑤, go straight ahead to the cycleway and back across the river to the car park. From its end by the 'artist's easel' go left through the gate. Follow the path to the road and turn right for 200yds (183m).

Turn right and follow a lane past **Halton Park** (Point Ⓐ). Continue for 275yds (251m) then go right up the track to **Hawkshead farm**. Just before the first barn go left. Skirt the farm, pass a marker post, and cross a stile by a tree on the skyline. Go left along the hedge then keep straight on and through a wood.

Descend to a stream then go up to **Lower Highfield**. From a signpost take the left of two tracks then follow the edge of the field above. Continue, by a high stone wall, to **Middle Highfield** (Point Ⓑ).

Go left into the farmyard and down the left side of the first house. Keep straight on, between two more houses, then follow a tall hedge over the highest of the high fields. The ground falls away, giving a great view up the valley.

Aim right of **Far Highfield**, to a stile. Descend rightwards to a footbridge. From another stile slant down to a stile alongside a gate, overlooking Aughton. Bear left, above the line of trees, to the road. Descend into the village and straight across the 'crossroads'.

Aughton is the home of the largest pudding in the world. Every 21 years, since 1824 and probably earlier, the villagers produce a colossal plum pudding – the 1992 version weighed 5,000lb (2,270kg). All because a boiler, used to soften willow wands for basket making, resembled 'a gert puddin boiler'.

The lane descends steeply then a track continues, past **Aughton Barns** (Point Ⓒ), towards the River Lune. Veer away from the river bank at a small marker post, towards a prominent white gate. Follow the slightly higher ground – the former river bank – to **Over Lune Barn**. Follow the river bank round the rest of the great bend until it swings sharply back left. Where the river meets the steep wooded slope, go up to a stile and some steps. A narrow but clear path runs through **Lawson's Wood**. At the far end, the waterworks bridge is seen just ahead. Go through the 'tunnel' and rejoin Walk 43 at Point ⑦.

# Glasson and Cockersands

*A very easy walk, at its most atmospheric on a blustery day.*

| | |
|---|---|
| •DISTANCE• | 5½ miles (8.8km) |
| •MINIMUM TIME• | 1hr 45min |
| •ASCENT / GRADIENT• | 82ft (25m) |
| •LEVEL OF DIFFICULTY• | |
| •PATHS• | Village streets, tow path, lanes, tracks and sea wall, 8 stiles |
| •LANDSCAPE• | Level fields, a wide estuary and rocky foreshore |
| •SUGGESTED MAP• | aqua3 OS Explorer 296 Lancaster, Morecambe & Fleetwood |
| •START / FINISH• | Grid reference: SD 446560 |
| •DOG FRIENDLINESS• | Grazing land, dogs need to be under close control |
| •PARKING• | Car park at East Quay, Glasson |
| •PUBLIC TOILETS• | Across road from car park |

## Walk 45 **Directions**

From the car park, go left along the edge of the harbour and continue up the canal, past the church to **Brows Bridge**.

It's immediately apparent that Glasson Dock is a working port, albeit on a modest scale, as well as being home to many pleasure craft. Lancaster itself, about 5 miles (8km) up the Lune, suffered a sharp decline in trade in the early 19th-century. The opening of the canal link to the sea at Glasson, in 1826, only partly stemmed the drop in the area's fortunes. Glasson is now a minor outpost of the Port of Lancaster, which centres on the deep-water harbour at Heysham.

> **WHERE TO EAT AND DRINK** ⓘ
>
> In addition to a café and a couple of pubs in the village itself, there's the highly-regarded **Stork** at Conder Green. You can walk there, along the old railway line, a return trip of about a mile (1.6km). There's well-kept ale and a good selection of food in hefty portions.

The Lancaster Canal never achieved its full economic potential because it was not linked to the rest of the national network. Ironically this is now set to change, with the development of a link at Preston.

Go up to the bridge and cross it. After 100yds (91m) fork left into **Jeremy Lane**. Just after a sharp double bend there's a footpath sign on the right over a culvert and through a gate. Follow the right field edge, round to the left and through a gate, over another culvert bridge and along an obvious track.

Go left at a junction along the lane to **Kendal Hill farm**. Just after the bungalow, but before the farm itself, cross a stile on the right, then another beside a drinking trough. Walk down past the farm to another culvert and continue straight ahead for about ½ mile (800m) over various footbridges and stiles. From a substantial bridge over a ditch, go straight ahead to a gap then along the side of the field towards **Crook Cottage**. The track alongside leads to the sea wall.

**Walk 45**

Go left, left again by **Lighthouse Cottage**, then right at the next junction. At the second sharp left-hand bend there's a gate on the right with a stile alongside. Follow the track to the farm, round past the house, and out to the ruins of **Cockersands Abbey**.

The site is most evocative on a wild day, but even then it's hard to imagine how isolated it must have been in the 12th century, when Hugh Garth, 'a hermit of great perfection', came here. It was then a virtual island. Erosion has pushed the shoreline closer while the marshes, which then stretched several miles inland, have now been drained – you've just walked across them. The site was relatively safe from marauders and well-removed from worldly temptation. It subsequently became a hospital and then a Premonstratensian priory. The only standing building is based on the Chapter House. A few other fragments of masonry remain.

From the ruins, walk out to the sea wall. If the tide's not too high it is worth venturing on to the foreshore, where you may find great drifts of mussel and cockle shells. These shellfish are still harvested commercially in Morecambe Bay.

About ¼ mile (400m) out, at the mouth of the Lune channel, is a small lighthouse. This still works, for the benefit of those craft which use the Lune channel. These are relatively few and it's much more probable that you'll see container ships or the Isle of Man ferry heading to or from Heysham, beyond the low spit of Sunderland Point. The harbour itself is just beyond the obvious and unsightly nuclear power stations.

**WHAT TO LOOK FOR**

Apart from Tithebarn Hill, and that's hardly a mountain, you might think this walk was completely flat. In fact variations in height of just a few feet were immensely significant before the marshes were drained. The abbey for instance, stands about 15ft (5m) above its surroundings. Other names – Kendal Hill, Thursland Hill, Bank Houses – also record the significance of **higher ground**.

Turn right along the sea wall, which brings you back to the junction by **Lighthouse Cottage**. Retrace the short section to **Crook Cottage** but continue to **Crook Farm**. Turn right just before the houses and along a track. After a gate on a bridge it becomes little more than tractor ruts as it swings towards a line of hawthorns, then becomes clearer again. Continue alongside a caravan site, then a lane leads out to a road. Go left and up to **Tithebarn Hill**.

There's no sign of a tithe barn today, but this is the highest point of the walk at 60ft (18m). The view indicator isn't as easy to read as it once was but it's clear enough. And isn't it good to know that Coniston Old Man is 27¾ miles (44.6km) away (especially if you can't see it)?

Directly opposite, at the mouth of the river, is Sunderland. The road to the village still floods at high tides. Turn right down **Tithe Barn Hill** into the village and across the swing bridge or lock gates. The car park's just beyond, on the right.

**WHILE YOU'RE THERE**

**Glasson** itself is worth a little more time: there's usually something going on in the outer harbour or the inner yacht basin. There's also a gallery/craft shop and, round the corner, the Smokehouse offers a wide range of delicacies.

# Down to the Summit on Clougha Pike

*A wild walk to a deceptive 'summit', which proves an unrivalled viewpoint overlooking the sweeping Bowland Fells.*

| | |
|---|---|
| •**DISTANCE**• | 5¼ miles (8.4km) |
| •**MINIMUM TIME**• | 2hrs |
| •**ASCENT / GRADIENT**• | 1,050ft (320m) ▲▲ ▲ ▲ |
| •**LEVEL OF DIFFICULTY**• | 🚶🚶 🚶🚶 🚶🚶 |
| •**PATHS**• | Mostly very rough moorland, sometimes rocky, 5 stiles |
| •**LANDSCAPE**• | Moorland with some rocky outcrops, above green valley |
| •**SUGGESTED MAP**• | aqua3 OS Explorer OL41 Forest of Bowland & Ribblesdale |
| •**START / FINISH**• | Grid reference: SD 526604 |
| •**DOG FRIENDLINESS**• | Access Area – dogs not permitted |
| •**PARKING**• | Access Area car park at Birk Bank |
| •**PUBLIC TOILETS**• | Nearest at Crook O'Lune (➤ Walk 43) |

## BACKGROUND TO THE WALK

Clougha Pike is the finest viewpoint in the Bowland Fells, possibly in the whole of Lancashire. There's lots to see at closer quarters too and the walk is always rewarding, but on a clear day it's nothing short of magnificent. Although the ground is sometimes very rough, the ascent is rarely very steep and the views expand with every stride.

### The Ridge of Clougha

The opening stages are almost level. After crossing the little aqueduct called Ottergear Bridge, the route swings round and climbs a little, then drops into a small, sharp-cut valley. This is the first of several curious channels, some of which cut right through the ridge of Clougha. These are relics from the end of the ice age. The edge of the ice sheet was stationary for a while in this area, dammed up behind the ridge. Torrents of meltwater pouring off the ice, and probably sometimes running underneath it, carved the network of channels. The most striking example is Windy Clough, seen near the end of the walk.

### Heather Moorland

Now the walk begins its steady ascent across the broad flanks. Apart from a few wet patches marked by rushes and cotton grass, the dominant vegetation is heather and bilberry. Heather moorland is widespread in Britain but rare in most of the rest of Europe. Geology, climate and soils are partly responsible, but the management of the land is equally significant. Controlled burning of areas of moor encourages the heather to produce new shoots, the main food for the red grouse. Like it or not, grouse shooting for sport is part of the ecology of these moors.

When the rocky crest of the ridge is reached, the climbing is over. The last stretch is generally level and when the summit of Clougha appears it definitely is slightly below you. This hardly detracts from the view, even though a sector is blocked by the higher ground of Grit Fell and beyond it Ward's Stone, the highest summit in Lancashire.

### Distant Views

The old trig point now bears a new view indicator, which will help you identify what you're looking at. The Clwydian Hills in Wales are apparent much more often than the higher, but more distant, peaks of Snowdonia. The distinctive profile of the Isle of Man, over 60 miles (97km) away in the Irish Sea, is also visible on a clear day. However, what grabs most of the attention is the sweep of the Lakeland skyline and the continuation of high ground eastwards, over the Howgill Fells and into Yorkshire, where the Three Peaks of Whernside, Ingleborough and Pen-y-ghent are dominant.

As you descend, the nick of Little Windy Clough appears over your right shoulder, and then the much deeper Windy Clough appears. The stream draining Windy Clough runs underground where we cross it but surfaces again a little lower down.

**Walk 46**

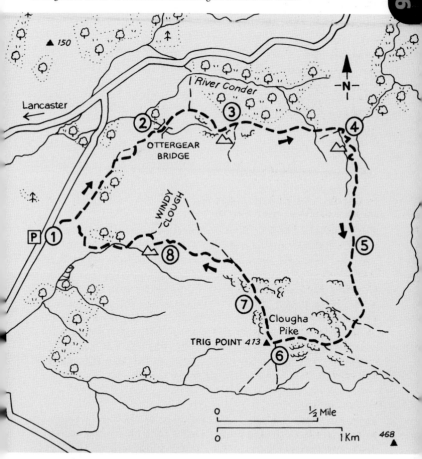

## Walk 46 Directions

① Follow the track above the car park, then fork left. It becomes a green path, running generally level, to **Ottergear Bridge**.

② Turn left and walk along a level track, then bear right at the next junction. The track climbs slightly, descends into a narrow valley, then climbs steeply up the far side before it finally eases and swings round to the right.

**WHERE TO EAT AND DRINK** ⓘ
**Woody's tea wagon** (► Walk 43) is as handy as anything, and **Lancaster** (► Walk 50) is just over the hill too. Alternatively, especially if you're heading southward, the **Fleece Inn**, on a crossroads just outside Dolphinholme, is an unpretentious but welcoming place, with a pleasant local feel despite its slightly isolated position. There's a small beer garden, a very cosy public bar and a dining room.

③ Go left on a narrow path, running almost level above a steeper slope. After 500yds (457m), it angles back down into the valley. Follow the base of the steep slope and cross a small stream. After 30yds (27m) a green track climbs to the right.

④ Wind up steeply to near-level moor. The path follows a slight groove, then skirts leftward around a boggy patch. The grassy path ahead is initially very faint. Keep just left of the continuous heather and it soon becomes clearer. There's another grooved section then a clear stony path rises leftward across steeper ground.

⑤ As the slope eases the path remains clear, passing a few sketchy cairns, then a 'Limit of Access Area' sign. Follow a groove, through or past tumbledown shooting butts. As the ground levels, trend right past cairns and marker stakes to an ugly new track. Cross and follow a thin grassy path with more marker stakes. Bear right up a slight rise and join a wider path at a cairn. Go right on a broad ridge, crossing a fence, to the summit trig point.

⑥ Descend a clear path on the right past a large cairn. There's a steep drop near by on the left, with some small crags. A fence converges from the right, eventually meeting a well-built wall.

⑦ Scramble down rocks by the end of the wall. Continue down its left side for about 300yds (274m). Bear left at a levelling above scattered boulders. Descend through a gap flanked by wrinkled rocks then across gentler slopes to a gate by the corner of a wall.

**WHILE YOU'RE THERE** ⓘ
In view from the summit, **Lancaster University** has various facilities open to the public, including its sports centre (the swimming pool might be a good way to unwind after the walk). On the cultural side it offers the Peter Scott Gallery and the Ruskin Library, a striking new building which contains a collection devoted to Victorian writer, artist and aesthete John Ruskin, an important figure if you're interested in landscape.

⑧ Head straight down until the ground steepens, then swing right and weave down towards **Windy Clough**. From a stile go left down a grooved path to an area of young trees. Fork left, closer to the stream, rejoining wetter alternative routes above larger oaks. Descend through gorse then follow duckboards skirting a bog. Turn right along a track then keep left over a slight rise to the car park.

**WHAT TO LOOK FOR** ⓘ
The red grouse is found only on the heather moors of northern Britain, but here they are plentiful. They often look black, apart from red 'eyebrows', but in good light a deep reddish-brown hue is apparent. Grouse will rise suddenly from close underfoot, with a loud whirr of wings and frantic alarm calls. It's hard to tell whether they're more startled than you are, or vice versa.

Walk 47

# Over the Underground: Leck Beck and Easegill Kirk

*A brief glimpse of the subterranean mysteries of limestone and a lot of fine wild country.*

| | |
|---|---|
| •DISTANCE• | 7½ miles (12.1km) |
| •MINIMUM TIME• | 3hrs |
| •ASCENT / GRADIENT• | 968ft (295m) ▲▲▲ |
| •LEVEL OF DIFFICULTY• | 🐾🐾 🐾🐾 🐾🐾 |
| •PATHS• | Field paths, indefinite moorland paths, quiet road, 3 stiles |
| •LANDSCAPE• | Sheltered river valley, wild moorland, gorge and pot-holes |
| •SUGGESTED MAP• | aqua3 OS Explorer OL2 Yorkshire Dales – Southern & Western |
| •START / FINISH• | Grid reference: SD 643767 |
| •DOG FRIENDLINESS• | Dogs should be on leads |
| •PARKING• | Park by Leck church (honesty box) |
| •PUBLIC TOILETS• | Nearest are at Devil's Bridge, Kirkby Lonsdale, 2 miles (3.2km) up A65 |

## BACKGROUND TO THE WALK

Yes, this is still Lancashire. A long wedge of countryside squeezed between Cumbria and North Yorkshire, with the highest ground in the county along the borders, reaching 2,251ft (686m) on Crag Hill. But it hardly feels like Lancashire: the landscape, with its limestone gorges, scars and pot-holes, is what you expect of the Yorkshire Dales.

### High Drama

The crucial thing about limestone is that it dissolves in water far more readily than other rocks. It can produce gentle beauty, as around Silverdale (► Walk 48), or it can yield high drama, as it does here. First, however, there's a lengthy preamble, following Leck Beck from green pastures to open moors, where you're as likely to see hen harriers as other walkers.

The drama begins with the gorge of Easegill Kirk. You can enter both its upper and lower reaches, though a vertical rock step blocks the direct connection between the two. The lower section of the gorge is particularly impressive, with leaning rock walls punctured by several cave entrances.

### Limestone Caves and Gaping Holes

Most of these are gloomy passages, which many people will find uninviting if not actually repellent, though you can see evidence of digging undertaken by cavers to enlarge the entrances. At the back, just to the right of the rock step, is another cave, which you can safely look into. Some extra light enters from a slot high on the left.

It's back into the open on the wide moors above Easegill Kirk. Initially there are only faint sheep tracks to follow, but you soon pick up an old wall and then an improving path. But the drama's not over, as the level moor is pockmarked with holes, from shallow pits to gaping shafts. Fortunately all the dangerous ones are fenced off. The most blatant is

Rumbling Hole. It gets its name from the constant sound – actually more of a tapping – of water striking stones at the bottom, 360ft (110m) down. Short Drop Cave is less spectacular, with a narrow entrance where the stream can normally be heard not far below.

Lost John's Cave, near the road, is the most important to cavers because of the extent of its underground passages. Further down, where the road runs in a slight valley, there's a small entrance right by the road, normally covered and bridged by scaffolding poles from where cavers start their descent.

Even if you normally hate road walking, the finish of this walk should win you over. The grass verges are kind to your feet and you'll often go the whole way without meeting a single car. Wide views stretch over Morecambe Bay and the Lake District at first, but as you lose height the perspective changes and increasingly it's a Lune Valley view.

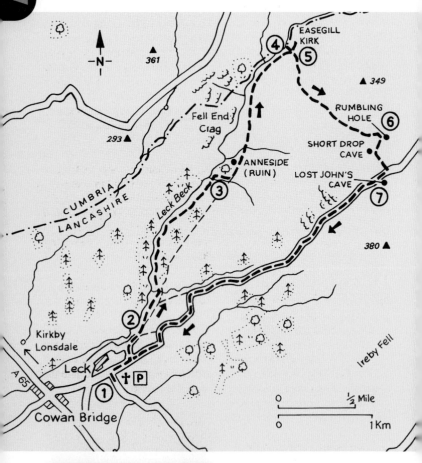

## Walk 47 Directions

① Turn right on the road then right again. Turn left by a post-box and go down a lane, bearing right at the bottom.

② At the end of the tarmac take the lower, left track to a stile then continue on a good tractor track. Just after crossing a stream the track divides. Go left through a gate into a wood then continue through a long pasture, passing a small

Walk 47

wooden house. Clamber over a stile at the far end. The track descends almost to river level then climbs away again.

③ Climb fairly steeply for about 300yds (274m) then go left in a slight dip past the ruins of **Anneside**. The path, now little more than a sheep track, runs fairly level and fairly straight until it meets a ruined wall. Cross the dip of a small stream then bear left out of it, crossing damp ground on to a grassy shoulder. Follow the crest of steeper slopes dropping towards the beck to arrive at the brink of a tree-filled gorge.

**WHERE TO EAT AND DRINK**
There are no facilities at Leck. You can get tea, coffee and soft drinks at **Cowan Bridge** but for meals and alcohol go straight across the A65 and 2 miles (3.2km) down a narrow twisting lane to the **Highwayman** at Nether Burrow, on the A683. There's plenty of room indoors and out.

④ Go straight ahead on a narrow path across the slope. It's not difficult, but it's clearly no place to slip. This leads into the upper reaches of **Easegill Kirk**. Look around, then retrace to the crossroads and descend to a more level area below some small outcrops. Cross a steep grass slope into the gorge. After exploring this return once more to the crossroads.

⑤ Now take the uphill footpath. Where it levels off go sharp right on a narrow track to a ruined wall. Follow this up to the left then along, above some rocky outcrops to a green conical pit. Keep trending upwards and to the right, on sheep tracks, to meet a long, straight, dry-stone wall. Follow this up to the left

**WHILE YOU'RE THERE**
**Kirkby Lonsdale**, just up the A65, is an old stone-built market town full of nooks and crannies. It has been widely used for film and TV locations. It's best known for its church, parts of which are Norman, and for Ruskin's View, just beyond the churchyard. Just outside the town is Devil's Bridge, an elegant medieval structure, below which are limestone outcrops and deep pools in the Lune.

to a clearer path. Several fenced holes now appear in a shallow dip in the moor. Bear left to the nearest one, then follow a narrow footpath past the second and third. Follow a shallow valley with no permanent stream, past several small sink holes to the deep shaft known as **Rumbling Hole**.

⑥ Turn right on a faint footpath across level moorland to another fenced hole, about 200yds (183m) away, called **Short Drop Cave**. From this head back towards the dry-stone wall and, just before reaching it, head up to the left to join the road. Turn right down it. After 150yds (137m) **Lost John's Cave** can be seen away to your left.

⑦ Continue walking down the quiet road for another 2½ miles (4km) back to **Leck**. Finally turn left near the church to return to the start of the walk.

**WHAT TO LOOK FOR**
Large-scale features like caves and gorges are one result of limestone wearing away in water, but it also produces distinctive features on a smaller scale. Many outcrops are marked by runnels and flutings, and level surfaces often form expanses of **limestone pavement**. These may appear flat from a distance, but the action of rain water often produces deep cracks.

# A Quart in a Pint Pot: Around Silverdale

*An easy-going walk, yet fascinating with its continuous changes of scenery.*

| | |
|---|---|
| **•DISTANCE•** | 5½ miles (8.8km) |
| **•MINIMUM TIME•** | 2hrs |
| **•ASCENT / GRADIENT•** | 426ft (130m) ▲▲▲ |
| **•LEVEL OF DIFFICULTY•** | 🚶🚶 🚶🚶 🚶 |
| **•PATHS•** | Little bit of everything, 10 stiles |
| **•LANDSCAPE•** | Pot-pourri of woodland, pasture, village lanes and shoreline |
| **•SUGGESTED MAP•** | aqua3 OS Explorer OL7 The English Lakes (SE) |
| **•START / FINISH•** | Grid reference: SD 471759 |
| **•DOG FRIENDLINESS•** | Can run free on shore and in woods |
| **•PARKING•** | Small National Trust car park for Eaves Wood |
| **•PUBLIC TOILETS•** | In Silverdale village |

## BACKGROUND TO THE WALK

The Arnside–Silverdale Area of Outstanding Natural Beauty (AONB) is barely longer than its name, yet intricate and exquisite. Unfortunately – for this book, anyway – half of it is in Cumbria. This walk attempts the impossible, to sample all of its delights in one go.

### A Mosaic of Habitats

The AONB covers a mere 29 square miles (75sq km) yet includes rocky coastline, salt marsh, wetland, pasture, woodland, heathland, crags and quarries, and some attractive villages, principally Silverdale in Lancashire and Arnside in Cumbria. With such a mosaic of habitats, it's no surprise that the area is rich in wildlife – more than half of all British flowering plant species are found here.

There's a fine start, through Eaves Wood with its yew trees and impressive beech ring, then the route sidles through the back lanes of Silverdale before reaching the coast. The channels of Morecambe Bay shift over time and so does the shoreline. The band of salt marsh around the Cove has shrunk drastically in the last few years. In future it may become more difficult to follow the shore, at least at high tide. (Fortunately the footpath across The Lots, just above, offers a ready-made alternative.)

### By the Sea

The described route avoids a tricky section of the coast south of Silverdale, returning to the shore near Jenny Brown's Point. The breakwater running out to sea recalls a failed 19th-century land reclamation scheme. Just around the corner stands the tall chimney of a copper smelting mill that operated around 200 years ago.

After Heald Brow comes Woodwell, the first of three 'wells' (actually springs) on the walk. At Woodwell the water issues from the crag above the square pool. This was used for watering cattle but now you're more likely to see dragonflies. Woodwell and the other 'wells' around Silverdale are found where the water-permeable limestone is interrupted by a band of impermeable material such as clay. Rainfall generally sinks quickly into limestone and there are no surface streams over most of the area, so the springs were of vital importance. This rapid drainage also means that relatively few of the footpaths are persistently muddy, even after heavy rain.

Lambert's Meadow, however, is usually damp. It sits in a hollow where fine wind-blown silt (known as loess) accumulated after the last ice age. The soil is dark and acidic, very different from that formed on the limestone, and the plant community is different too.

# Walk 48 Directions

① From the end of the National Trust car park at Eaves Wood, follow the footpath to a T-junction.

Go right a few paces then left, climbing gently. Keep left to the beech ring, then straight on. Descend through a complex junction to a high wall and continue on this line to a lane.

② Cross on to a track signed 'Cove Road'. Keep ahead down a narrow path (**Wallings Lane**), a drive, another track and another narrow path to a wider road. After 200yds (183m) go left down **Cove Road**.

③ From the Cove walk leftward, below the cliffs, to the shore. Walk up the road to **Beach Garage** then take the footpath alongside.

> **WHAT TO LOOK FOR**  ⓘ
>
> If you do this walk in winter, you'll see huge flocks of **wading birds** around the shoreline. Morecambe Bay is an internationally important site for migrants and over-wintering birds. In spring listen, rather than look, for the rare bittern. This relative of the heron is rarely seen but its *booming* courtship call – like someone blowing across the top of a milk bottle – can be heard up to a mile (1.6km) away.

> **WHILE YOU'RE THERE**  ⓘ
>
> The **Leighton Moss RSPB reserve** and nearby Leighton Hall are obvious attractions, but for something different (and free) pop in to **Trowbarrow Quarry**. Last worked in 1959, the quarry is now a Local Nature Reserve, and it's also a Site of Special Scientific Interest (SSSI) for its geology. Most striking is the near-vertical Main Wall, basically an upturned slice of fossil sea-bed. Trowbarrow is also very popular with rock climbers.

④ At the next road turn right for 600yds (549m) then bear right down **Gibraltar Lane** for 350yds (320m). Enter the National Trust property of **Jack Scout**.

⑤ Descend left to the limekiln then follow a narrowing path directly away from it. This swings left above a steep drop and descends. Follow a broad green path to a gate. After 100yds (91m), another gate leads into the lane. At its end bear left below **Brown's Houses**. Follow the edge of the salt marsh to a stile, go up slightly, then along to a signpost.

⑥ Turn left, climbing steeply to an awkward squeeze stile. The gradient eases, over rock and through a lightly wooded area into the open. Go left to a stile then follow a wall down and into a small wood. Follow a track down right. Cross

the road to a gap in the wall, descend, then walk below the crags to **Woodwell**.

⑦ The path signed 'The Green via cliff path' leads to a rocky staircase. At the top go straight ahead to join a broader path. Follow it left, slant right, then continue into woodland. A stile on the right and a narrow section lead to a road. Go right 100yds (91m), then left into **The Green**. Keep right at a junction then join a wider road.

⑧ Go left for 75yds (69m) then right, signposted 'Burton Well Lambert's Meadow'. The track soon descends then swings left, passing **Burton Well** on the right. Cross a stile into **Lambert's Meadow**, then go right, over a footbridge to a gate. Climb up, with some steps, and continue more easily to a fork. Go left alongside a pool (**Bank Well**) into a lane. Go left and at the end the car park is virtually opposite.

> **WHERE TO EAT AND DRINK**  ⓘ
>
> The tea room at **Wolf House Gallery** is a great spot for mid-walk refreshments, as long as you can find a table. For post-walk celebrations, head for the **New Inn** in the nearby village of Yealand Conyers. There's good food and beer, a small cosy bar, a non-smoking dining room and a walled beer garden that's delightful on summer evenings.

# To Leighton Moss

*A gallon in a quart pot – the diversity of Arnside–Silverdale in one shot.*
**See map and information panel for Walk 48**

| | |
|---|---|
| •DISTANCE• | 8½ miles (13.7km) |
| •MINIMUM TIME• | 3hrs |
| •ASCENT / GRADIENT• | 837ft (255m) ▲▲▲ |
| •LEVEL OF DIFFICULTY• | 杁 杁 杁 |

## Walk 49 Directions
## (Walk 48 option)

At the signpost (Point ⑥) go right
to follow the embankment. Cross
the sluice at the end then go left
under the railway and out to the
road (Point Ⓐ). Fields on the right
are being restored to wetland. Turn
right along the road for 300yds
(274m) then left up **Crag Road**.

After 600yds (549m) there's a track
on the left. Follow it for ½ mile
(800m) to a gate on the right with a
sign 'Concessionary Path Warton
Crag'. A green path rises gently
through open woodland, then
another gate leads into thicker
woods. The trees obscure any
obvious sign of the Iron-Age hill
fort that once existed here.

Go straight on at a signpost, past
the beacon, until the view opens
out above **Warton Crag** (Point Ⓑ).
The panorama extends from the
Bowland Fells, over Morecambe
Bay, to the Lakeland skyline.

Return to the signpost and bear
right. After 400yds (366m) fork
right by a split boulder and descend
a rock cutting into a tree-filled
bowl. Fork left as the gradient eases

then descend again in a shallow
trough. At the bottom, near a wall,
go left. The path roughly follows the
wall then meets a stony track.
Descend this to the road.

Go left, straight up for 700yds
(640m), then swinging right. About
250yds (229m) past the gates of
**Leighton Hall** there's a footpath on
the left that has been made
wheelchair-accessible. Follow it to
**Summerhouse Hill** (Point Ⓒ),
overlooking Leighton Hall.

Descend to the curve of the drive by
the Hall then fork right into a
walled lane. Follow this for ½ mile
(800m) to **Grisedale farm**. Roughly
100yds (91m) further on, fork right
and join the causeway across
**Leighton Moss**. Halfway along is
the public hide (Point Ⓓ).

At the end go right on the road for
150yds (137m) then cross to a gate.
Cross the golf course via a couple of
guide posts to a belt of woodland.
Cross the track to a path winding
through the overgrown outworks of
**Trowbarrow Quarry**. Cross the
track again by an information
board, go down a path and cross
the railway. From the white gate go
right to a lane. Go left, then right.
At the next junction go left on **Park
Road** back to the car park.

**Walk 50**

# Time-honoured Lancaster

*A castle, historic waterfront and attractive streets in Lancashire's finest town.*

| | |
|---|---|
| •DISTANCE• | 3 miles (4.8km) |
| •MINIMUM TIME• | 1hr |
| •ASCENT / GRADIENT• | 262ft (80m) ▲▲▲ |
| •LEVEL OF DIFFICULTY• | 🏃🏃🏃 |
| •PATHS• | City streets, paths with setts, canal tow path |
| •LANDSCAPE• | Basically urban, but with good leavening of open space |
| •SUGGESTED MAP• | aqua3 OS Explorer 296 Lancaster, Morecambe & Fleetwood |
| •START / FINISH• | Grid reference: SD 474619 |
| •DOG FRIENDLINESS• | Can run free on tow path, care needed on busy roads |
| •PARKING• | Parksafe at Mitre House, northbound on one-way system |
| •PUBLIC TOILETS• | At car park and in city centre |

## Walk 50 Directions

Exit from the car park to a cobbled haven alongside a busy road. In front is **Covell Cross** and above it the Judge's Lodgings. This lovely 17th-century house now houses a furniture museum and a museum of childhood. Go up, with the **Judge's Lodgings** on your right, on to **Castle Hill**.

Shakespeare's phrase 'Time-honoured Lancaster' originally described not a city but a man, John O'Gaunt, second Duke of Lancaster. The imposing gateway known as John O'Gaunt's Gate was built during the reign of his son, Henry IV. Walk up to its left, then round behind the castle to the visitor entrance.

Large parts of the castle are still in use as a prison, while the remainder also houses lawcourts. When these are not in session tours take in the courtrooms, the ancient dungeons, the magnificent Shire Hall and the Drop Room, where the condemned

awaited execution – among them the Pendle Witches (▶ Walk 33). Go through the gateway into the Priory churchyard. (A short detour rightwards gives a fine view over the city.) The church is among the finest in Lancashire, one of its most notable features being the superb 14th-century choir stalls. From the west front of the church, walk down a narrow path (known as **Vicarage Lane**). Half-way down a sign points right to the slightly disappointing Roman bathhouse remains.

Return to Vicarage Lane, descend steps, cross a cycleway/footpath and continue down the last bit of Vicarage Lane to **Saint George's Quay**. Turn left and walk about 300yds (274m) to the **Maritime Museum**. This lovely old building

### WHILE YOU'RE THERE ⓘ

You can't miss the **Ashton Memorial**, crowning the ridge east of the city. (It's equally conspicuous, and often puzzling, to travellers on the M6.) Variously called 'the Taj Mahal of the North' and 'England's grandest folly', it was built between 1906 and 1908.

was originally the Customs House, built in 1764, during the relatively brief period when Lancaster was a major port.

Return along the riverside towards the prominent **Millennium Bridge** (no prizes for guessing when it was constructed). Walk up the ramp on to the bridge, go right, then bear left along the old railway line. Reaching the main road, slope off right and through the underpass. Emerging on to the open grassy **Green Ayre**, bear left and walk up beside the river to admire **Skerton Bridge**. Completed in 1788, the bridge is notable as the first bridge in England with a level roadway.

> ### WHERE TO EAT AND DRINK ⓘ
> Lancaster is crammed with pubs and eateries. In the city centre the **Blue Anchor** is probably the best of several pubs. The **Sun Café** (in Sun Street) has bistro food and plays great jazz.

Turn around then bear left towards the traffic-light. Cross the street on your left, turn right and cross again when lights permit. Go up steps into a car park. Leave by the vehicle exit then cross the road above and go up the street almost opposite. Turn left into **De Vitre Street**, second right into **Shaw Street** and through a gap at its end.

Turn right along the canal tow path. Several cotton mills still stand, though they now serve other functions. Go under two bridges and below the grand Roman Catholic **Cathedral**, designed by the Lancaster firm of Paley and Austin.

At the third bridge the tow path changes sides, by a spiral ramp that allowed horses to cross without being unhitched. Continue past the

**White Cross** pub. The White Cross complex originally produced oilcloth but now houses a wide variety of educational, office and light industrial activities. Continue under another bridge then cross by the new footbridge just before the **Water Witch**.

Cross the road into **Queen Street** – another collection of good Georgian houses – and down to **Queen Square**. Bear left along the main road for 100yds (91m) to a pedestrian crossing, then turn right down **Common Garden Street**. At Marks and Spencer turn left into pedestrianised **Penny Street**. At **Horseshoe Corner**, turn left up **Market Street** to Market Square. The City Museum here was formerly the town hall, built in 1781 and replaced by a much more grandiose but less beautiful one (off the walk route) in 1909. There are some very good displays upstairs that tell much more about the history of the area.

Continue past the entrance to **New Street** then look for a narrow entry (Music Room Passage) on the right, which leads into **Music Room Square**, named for the enigmatic building at the back. Follow Sun Street to its end and turn left up **Church Street**. The pedestrian crossing at the top returns you to **Covell Cross**.

> ### WHAT TO LOOK FOR ⓘ
> Half-way down **Penny Street**, coins are embedded in the pavement. The street is actually named for one Thomas Penny, but never mind. At **Horseshoe Corner**, there's still a horseshoe set into the paving. It's supposed to be where John O'Gaunt's horse cast a shoe, but it's more likely that it marks the site of ancient horse fairs.

# Walking in Safety

All these walks are suitable for any reasonably fit person, but less experienced walkers should try the easier walks first. Route finding is usually straightforward, but you will find that an Ordnance Survey map is a useful addition to the route maps and descriptions.

### Risks

Although each walk here has been researched with a view to minimising the risks to the walkers who follow its route, no walk in the countryside can be considered to be completely free from risk. Walking in the outdoors will always require a degree of common sense and judgement to ensure that it is as safe as possible.

- Be particularly careful on cliff paths and in upland terrain, where the consequences of a slip can be very serious.

- Remember to check tidal conditions before walking on the seashore.

- Some sections of route are by, or cross, busy roads. Take care and remember traffic is a danger even on minor country lanes.

- Be careful around farmyard machinery and livestock, especially if you have children with you.

- Be aware of the consequences of changes in the weather and check the forecast before you set out. Carry spare clothing and a torch if you are walking in the winter months. Remember the weather can change very quickly at any time of the year, and in moorland and heathland areas, mist and fog can make route finding much harder. Don't set out in these conditions unless you are confident of your navigation skills in poor visibility. In summer remember to take account of the heat and sun; wear a hat and carry spare water.

- On walks away from centres of population you should carry a whistle and survival bag. If you do have an accident requiring the emergency services, make a note of your position as accurately as possible and dial 999.

# Acknowledgements

Doing the walks is the easy part. Loneliness is never a problem on the hills, but it's always good to have the right company, and I'm grateful to Bernie for accompanying me whenever she could. I'm even more grateful for all her support and encouragement during the infinitely harder and lonelier processes of research and writing. I must also thank my parents for many things, not least starting me in Cheshire and then moving to Lancashire later on! My brother Richard gave good advice on the Cheshire walks. Finally, thanks to John, Dennis and Chris.

**AQUA3** AA Publishing and Outcrop Publishing Services would like to thank Chartech for supplying aqua3 maps for this book.
For more information visit their website: www.aqua3.com.

**Series management:** Outcrop Publishing Services Limited, Cumbria
**Series editor:** Chris Bagshaw
**Front cover:** AA Photo Library/M Trelawney